ghost hunt

true new zealand ghost stories

julie miller and grant osborn

REED

For Jo and Karen, for their patience
and long-distance love ...

Front cover: The 'melting corridor' photograph taken at Waitomo Caves Hotel, an epicentre of paranormal activity.
Back cover: The wispy figure of the Pink Lady, a phantom residing in an abandoned hospital just outside a major North Island city, photographed here in 2004.

our nation. our voice.

Published by Reed Books, a division of Reed Publishing (NZ) Ltd, 39 Rawene Road, Birkenhead, Auckland 10. Associated companies, branches and representatives throughout the world.

© 2005 Julie Miller and Grant Osborn/TVNZ
The authors assert their moral rights in the work.

ISBN 0 7900 1012 7
First published 2005

National Library of New Zealand Cataloguing-in-Publication Data

Miller, Julie.
Ghost hunt : true New Zealand ghost stories / Julie Miller and
Grant Osborn.
Companion to the television series 'Ghost hunt'.
ISBN 0-7900-1012-7
1. Ghosts–New Zealand. 2. Haunted places–New Zealand.
I. Osborn, Grant. II. Ghost hunt (Television program) III. Title

Design by Cheryl Rowe

Printed in New Zealand

contents

preface

The idea behind *Ghost Hunt* is to present our search for evidence of the supernatural, and let the readers make up their own minds as to whether or not ghosts exist. This book, which delves a little deeper into the fascinating stories that lie behind true New Zealand hauntings, will hopefully not only provide hours of entertaining reading but give more insight into what lies beyond ...

acknowledgements

This book has been written with the support and cooperation of many people, including those who were involved in the making of the *Ghost Hunt* television series. We'd specifically like to thank Jane Wilson from TV2 for commissioning the television series; without her vision none of this would have been possible. Thanks also to Kathryn Graham, our commissioning editor, for her insight and sense of humour, and to Roger Masters at TVNZ Licensing for orchestrating the book to accompany the series.

We'd like to thank the staff and crew at Screentime, particularly Ross Jennings, Richard Browes, Pamela Cain and our researcher Angelique Kasmara, who was responsible for uncovering many of these stories and finding eyewitnesses who have had their own ghostly experiences. Also thanks to Phill Pendleton, our camera guru responsible for the amazing visual style of the series.

Thanks to the owners, staff and residents at the various locations who were willing to share their experiences, particularly Sophie Barker, Martin Sandifer, Graham Hemming and John Webster. To those who allowed us to film into the wee hours of the morning, thanks for putting up with us!

Special thanks to Dorothy O'Donnell from www.nzghosts.co.nz for allowing us to access the research and stories compiled on her website; Andrew Smith from

Dunedin's Hair Raiser Ghost Walk Tours; and David McGill for his fascinating history of the St James Theatre. Also thanks to Justine O'Gahdra-Sharp for her psychic wisdom and insights.

We'd like to give special acknowledgement to Mayor Bob Harvey from Waitakere City Council — thanks for being a master storyteller! Also to our other interviewees: Deborah from Larnach Castle; Yvonne, Luke and Lance from the hospital; Yule, Corey and Chris from the Fortune Theatre; Jude and Karen from St Bathans; Mary Roberts from Whatipu Lodge; Mary Gilligan and Arthur Smith from the Friends of Waikumete; and Keri from the Platform 7 cafe.

Of course, we must also acknowledge the investigative efforts of Carolyn Taylor and Michael Hallows, who dared to venture into dark and scary corners in search of ghosts of the past. Their enthusiasm, bravery and honesty helped make the *Ghost Hunt* series a pleasure to produce. Special thanks to fellow Aussie Brad Hills, the director of paranormal investigations, for leading the way and interpreting many of the findings. Thanks for being a whizz computer geek, comedian and all-round nice guy!

To the wonderful team at Reed Books, who have been so supportive and enthusiastic about this project — thanks for everything. Special thanks to Peter Dowling and our editor Sam Hill.

Finally, we'd like to thank our long-suffering families and friends who put up with us disappearing 'across the pond' to New Zealand for six months! Not that we're promising we won't do it again …

introduction

When we (a couple of Australian television producers) were invited by Television New Zealand (TVNZ) to make a local version of *Ghost Hunt*, we jumped at the opportunity. Not only did it present us with the chance to fulfil a long-standing dream, it was being offered in a country famed for its mythical, mystical qualities. This is the home of *Lord of the Rings*, *Heavenly Creatures* and *The Frighteners* after all ... surely, any nation that has produced an exponent of the horror-movie genre of the calibre of Peter Jackson would appreciate the entertainment potential of the supernatural realm.

These assumptions were well-founded and our excitement was justified, although as it turned out, isolating epicentres of paranormal activity in New Zealand was more difficult than we anticipated. For a start, there is little documented evidence of hauntings within New Zealand. The last book written on the subject was published in the 1970s (Robyn Jenkin's *The New Zealand Ghost Book*, Reed, 1978), and there is only one, albeit comprehensive and lovingly compiled, website dedicated to New Zealand's ghost stories (www.nzghosts.co.nz).

Many of the stories that we came across were anecdotal, in keeping with the rich oral tradition of the Maori people, who delight in tales of the unexplained. While these legends present a valuable insight into the history and beliefs of Maori, the ephemeral nature of the tales precluded documentation in a television programme such as ours.

This former morgue, situated on the grounds of an abandoned psychiatric hospital near Auckland, is the perfect location for paranormal activity.

For the purposes of filming *Ghost Hunt*, we required locations with a strong backstory — preferably a dark, tragic tale — as well as a well-documented history of paranormal activity. Eyewitnesses to these occurrences needed to be tracked down and evidence, whether verbal or photographic, compiled to add weight to our mission.

Each location needed to be large and complex enough to justify the presence of two investigators and, of course, scary in both appearance and atmosphere. On these grounds we had to dismiss such locations as tiny backcountry cabins and private residences — regardless of how compelling the evidence of hauntings was they could not have sustained an entire night of filming.

Interestingly, some commercial businesses, particularly high-profile hotels and tourist ventures, were nervous about admitting to their ghostly presences, claiming that exposure as a haunted site would be bad for business, particularly among their Asian clientele. Fortunately, other businesses. such as Larnach Castle (chapter 1) and the Waitomo Caves Hotel (chapter 3) embrace their ghostly past, and have owners, staff and customers who are happy to discuss their paranormal experiences. We were also lucky to encounter individuals, some of them high-profile public figures such as Waitakere City Mayor Bob Harvey, who were delighted to be able to share their experiences and talk about their belief in the supernatural realm (see chapter 6).

One of the unique features of the *Ghost Hunt* television series is its reliance on technology as an investigative tool. Rather than focusing on the psychic hunches of mediums or paranormal experts, we decided to take a scientific approach and utilise high-tech ghost-busting equipment designed to provide evidence of (as opposed to proving) paranormal activity.

Spearheading the investigations was one of New Zealand's foremost paranormal enthusiasts, Brad Hills, an Australian actor and presenter based in Auckland. With a background in editing, television production and computer graphic design, Brad's technical expertise was invaluable to the investigation, particularly with setting up and operating specialist cameras, complicated computer systems and ghost-hunting gadgets such as infra-red non-contact thermometers and electro-magnetic field (EMF) meters (see chapter 2).

Carolyn Taylor is a TVNZ presenter who made her mark in children's television on the popular series *What Now?* This was

[From left] The intrepid investigators on the hunt for New Zealand ghosts: Michael Hallows, team leader Brad Hills and Carolyn Taylor.

Carolyn's first venture into adult television, and it was a baptism of fire that placed her well outside her comfort zone. Coming from a spiritual background, Carolyn has a strong personal belief in the afterlife and had the odd paranormal experience during childhood. A self-confessed scaredy-cat, however, nothing could prepare her for the sheer terror she felt before each and every investigation. On most occasions it was simply being alone in the dark that freaked Carolyn out. But Carolyn also had to face the fact that she was, at times, in the presence of unseen forces. She has a tendency to hear noises all around her, noises that proved untraceable, as well as attract poltergeist activity such as falling pool cues, brooms and slamming doors. Carolyn also has the rare ability to detect coloured lights, which indicate a spiritual presence in her vicinity.

Meanwhile, actor Michael Hallows is a 'seeker' — a man on a quest to uncover evidence of paranormal activity. Bold and brave, Michael was predisposed to call or summon spirits into his presence and demand proof of their existence in the form of an apparition or a physical appearance. And on more than one occasion, Michael was buffered by an icy cold wind that would whirl and crash over him in a wave. He believes that this was a sign of a supernatural power revealing itself to him.

Filming the series took place over a six-week period in February and March 2005. The four stories from the South Island were investigated in one block; the others from the North Island were spread out to allow the small but hard-working production team to recover. Each episode was filmed in one long, and typically harrowing, night that commenced at around 3 p.m., with a camera crew covering the arrival of the team, developing the backstory, the technical set-up and interviews.

As darkness fell, the investigators would then venture forth on their own, scouting in and around the haunted location. During these walkthroughs, they were alone and unaccompanied by a camera crew, but everything was captured on the pre-set surveillance cameras or on specialist mini-DVs (digital video recorders) and handycams. Carolyn and Michael's facial emotions were registered via their helmets, a device that housed two cameras: one that was directed to show the investigator's line of sight, the other that looked back into their eyes. The extreme closeness of this angle left no room for doubt — uncontrollable fear registered as a rapid subconscious flickering of the eyeballs. And it manifested itself many times. Brad, in the meantime, monitored their movements via the surveillance system which fed back into the computer screens in the Ghostmobile. Brad often steered the explorers into areas at the location that reported fluctuations in temperature or electromagnetic fields.

The photo and video evidence collected during the investigations proved both intriguing and compelling. Of the many photographs taken on location by the *Ghost Hunt*

Each investigator wears a helmet device that houses two cameras: one that shows their line of vision, the other directed into their own face at an extreme angle to register conscious and subconscious manifestations of fear.

team, some revealed strange shapes and blurred figures that provoke real questions about paranormal activity. While these photographs in themselves do not prove undeniably the existence of ghosts, they do support the documented evidence of temperature drops, electromagnetic flux and, of course, the feelings of the investigators at the time. Added weight to the building body of evidence came from moving images captured on video of what appear to be orbs floating past a camera and a spectral face passing a window.

The question most commonly asked of us in regard to this project is the obvious one: 'Do you believe in ghosts?' After spending six intense months of our lives on this project, during which not one single member of the team — either behind or in front of the camera — failed to have at least one spooky, inexplicable experience, we came away with one indisputable insight. And it usually comprises our answer: 'Anything is possible ...'

1. larnach castle, near dunedin

On a remote and lonely hilltop outside Dunedin, among the steeply undulating countryside of the Otago Peninsula, Larnach Castle stands a silent sentinel. Aloof and foreboding, out of place, out of time, and very, very haunted, Larnach Castle is unique among New Zealand's supernatural sites in that the sources of its haunting are well-documented. And they centre on the misfortunes of one man, the man whose ghost is reported to forlornly stroll alongside the castle's parapet on bitterly cold and windy nights: William Larnach. The man who built the castle that would eventually lead to his downfall ...

With their dark histories, meandering hallways, spiralling stairwells, secret spaces and generally spooky atmosphere, castles create a setting ideal for a haunting. Larnach Castle might lack the bloody past of many of Europe's great castles but its dark story is soaked in sorrow, regret and anger — more than enough to spur restless spirits to stalk its chilly corridors. And the rise to glory and steep fall from grace of its principal spirit unfolds like a Shakespearean tragedy.

An ambitious man, William Larnach arrived in New Zealand in 1867 from Australia with a chip on his shoulder. His father, once a well-to-do member of the landed gentry, had fallen from grace both socially and financially. Fortunately, young Larnach was still well connected; his uncle Donald, as

It took 16 years to build Larnach Castle, one of New Zealand's most prominent supernatural sites with a dark, menacing history.

1/4-003226; F. Alexander Turnbull Library, Wellington.

the Chairman of the Bank of New South Wales, secured him a job as a bank clerk. While working his way up to branch manager, Larnach managed to secure the hand of a wealthy heiress, Eliza Jane Guise. With Uncle Donald pulling strings behind the scenes, Larnach was appointed chief manager of the Bank of Otago in 1867. On arriving in Dunedin with his new wife, he set upon lifting himself into the social stratum he felt to be his birthright (albeit with his wife's money). And what better way to initiate such a move than to build a castle?

It was a mammoth task. Construction of the 25-room neo-Gothic mansion — christened 'The Camp' by Larnach — took 16 years. During that period, Larnach established himself as a prominent business figure in Dunedin, at the time the largest city and leading industrial and financial centre of New Zealand. Larnach had his fingers in finance, farming, frozen meat, mining, timber, railroads and housing.

He also entered the political arena. As a Member of the House of Representatives he handled several major government portfolios, and along the way proving himself a poster boy for the abuse of public office. Fortunately for Larnach, an inflated opinion of his own business abilities (which proved negligible at best) were offset by his willingness to breach the trust of his government positions — especially when it came to wrangling land deals — in order to improve his own financial prospects.

But things, in general, were looking up. Larnach finally began to appear to others as the great, self-made man he always saw himself to be. And he made it clear to those around him that his efforts in New Zealand were nothing more than a stepping stone: the Antipodes were mere colonies and his ultimate aim was to move to England where he would live as a lord. From 1880 onwards, however, Larnach's fortunes began to topple like dominoes, each one splattering a huge dollop of hubris (or excessive pride and arrogance) on the way down ...

The first business misfortune occurred in the mid-1870s, when Larnach was compelled to leave the Bank of Otago under a very dark cloud. The London-registered National Bank of New Zealand had absorbed the financial institute, which till that time had been run as his personal fiefdom. Larnach had come under attack for misappropriation of funds by one of the bank's London directors; it seems that Larnach, as manager of the bank, had felt himself entitled to a hefty commission for acting as agent in securing finance for a local land deal involving an American businessman of equally dubious ethics.

In the late 1870s Larnach travelled to England, ostensibly to secure a loan for the New Zealand government but in actuality to offload rabbit-infested tracts of land at outrageously inflated prices to unsuspecting British investors via the public float of his own company, New Zealand Agricultural Co. On his return, Larnach was regularly overheard grumbling that he deserved a knighthood for his services to the Commonwealth during his two-year trip on the taxpayers' dollar. This sentiment came from a man who reportedly delighted in flaunting his superiority by whipping his buggy horses into a lather, sending pedestrians scurrying left and right as he thundered down Dunedin's George Street; a man who openly flouted the law of the land by holding illegal cockfights with cronies on his castle grounds ...

Larnach's first major personal misfortune occurred in 1880 when he was in Melbourne on business. During his absence, his wife Eliza Jane died from complications of an apoplectic fit. Bitterly blaming medical incompetence for her death, he seemed racked with remorse at the amount of time he had spent absent from The Camp. Yet, he quickly recovered to take a new wife — Mary, the half-sister of Eliza Jane — a little over a year later.

This union appears to have been a business arrangement more than a loving marriage, and went ahead despite the longstanding taboo against marrying again into the family of the deceased. The public float of the New Zealand Agricultural Co. had not gone well, and, unbeknown to Dunedin society, the mighty William Larnach was peering down the barrel of bankruptcy. In exchange for Mary's hand, Larnach offered to sign over all his private assets to her and so protect them from business insolvency. The move temporarily staved off bankruptcy, but Mary tragically died of a brain tumour less than five years later. Once again the doctors were to blame.

A few years later Larnach's favourite daughter from his first marriage, Kate, passed away from typhoid. Larnach was devastated. He had been so fond of Kate that he had built an enormous ballroom next to the castle for the sole purpose of hosting her twenty-first birthday celebrations. He could never bring himself to enter the room again.

And it went from bad to worse. The next business venture to turn turtle was Guthrie & Larnach's New Zealand Timber & Woodware Factories Co. (which had itself been plundered by Larnach to provide building materials for The Camp). Its collapse heralded the end of William Larnach as a business force in New Zealand. At this point he could have sold The Camp, moved into more modest surrounds, and continued to live quite comfortably, as a few of New Zealand's other failed buccaneering businessmen-cum-politicians of the time had done. But Larnach's inestimable vanity got the better of him, and he was loath to relinquish the

Although regal and extravagantly detailed inside and out, Larnach's own children seldom visited the castle as they found its atmosphere so remote and depressing.

status his beloved castle had brought him in Dunedin society.

His alternative strategy involved two foolish moves. The first was to invest virtually all of what was left of his funds in the newly formed Colonial Bank (of which he was a board member). The second was to take yet another bride, Constance de Bathe Brandon, over 20 years his junior.

The inhabitants of Larnach's intensely gloomy castle never found it a comfortable place to live, as architecturally impressive as it is. Despite breathtaking views of Otago Harbour and Port Chalmers, it was whipped by unforgiving winds and regularly enshrouded by fogs that could achieve the thickness of pea soup within minutes. Larnach's grown children, on returning from their education in Europe, eschewed visiting The Camp because they found its remoteness so depressing, and Larnach's demeanour became increasingly thorny.

As Larnach himself was spending more and more time away from his own castle, his young wife Constance felt increasingly isolated and lonely. She found solace in the arms of Larnach's youngest son, Douglas, and a torrid affair began. The journey from Dunedin to the castle took a whole day by buggy, and the expansive view from atop its tower allowed an easy opportunity to observe any imminent return of Larnach, so it seemed the castle was an ideal venue for just such an infidelity.

How the keeper of the castle found out about the affair conducted within his very own walls is not known. But Larnach did find out, and it sent him into an indignant rage and a deep depression.

Then, the final blow to a man renowned for his boundless ego, vanity and single-mindedness: the Colonial Bank foundered in the mid-1890s, and what remained of Larnach's fortune went down the drain with it. The cost of building his castle had been crippling and now even its upkeep was debilitating. For all intents and purposes, the king had lost his castle. He had lost all his businesses. He had lost his status in society. He had lost two wives to disease, and his deceitful third wife to his youngest son. All he had left was his position in Parliament ...

In late 1897 an embittered William Larnach travelled to Wellington to attend Parliament. At 5 p.m. on 12 October, after attending a parliamentary session, he wandered alone into Committee Room J. There he held a loaded pistol to his head and pulled the trigger. Approaching the end, he was unable to bear the thought of taking his life in the structure he had erected to honour his own greatness ...

Yet it would seem that the castle is exactly where his restless spirit is trapped, along with the other participants in the Larnach family tragedy. The demise of William Larnach marked the end of the castle's days as the family bastion. It was sold to the government by his son Donald who, stricken by guilt, likewise opted to shoot himself in the head. Donald's choice of venue was the Grand Hotel in Dunedin and his bleak suicide note requested that his ashes be 'taken out to sea and dumped overboard ... On no account have prayers read at my burial ... I absolutely disbelieve in the Bible.'

After the clearance sale of goods and chattels that had followed the castle's closure, the *Otago Witness* presciently declared, 'The once beautiful abode of the late Hon. Mr William Larnach will soon be an artistic ruin, the abode of morepokes [sic] and ghosts.'

In the ensuing years Larnach Castle underwent many

incarnations, as a mental hospital, a nunnery, a cabaret club, a military base for US soldiers during the Second World War, and, penultimately, as a derelict ruin.

It was during the years of dereliction that the castle gained infamy as a haunted house — a sad, formerly glorious ruin, symbol of lost dreams and frustrated ambitions, lurking miserably on the outskirts of town, the kind of place that seemed designed for teenagers to dare each other to enter at night. Over the years its legend and reputation as a place of mystery grew, as did the legion of ghost sightings. Countless intrepid trespassers have run, white-faced, from the premises — usually to recount an encounter with a dark, stocky figure in period garb and hat, gliding menacingly down is chilly corridors.

In 1967 Larnach Castle was purchased by Barry and Margaret Barker, who intended to restore it to its former glory. During the renovation, unexplained happenings were frequent, and Barry suspected the spirit of William Larnach might be involved. While the lawn was being mowed one still, windless day, a tree mysteriously came crashing down and crushed the mower. On a similarly calm day, a pane of glass inexplicably popped out of a pergola and shattered on the ground. Barry also had the strange sense that there was water somewhere under the castle grounds, and claimed it was as though the information was being passed on to him by a voice from the other side. Barry was directed by this guide to an area on the grounds and, kicking away at debris, uncovered a ringbolt. He lifted it only to uncover an enormous water tank, not marked on the castle plans, which had lain unused since the early days of Larnach.

Residual haunting

According to paranormal experts, there are two types of ghost; one is the manifestation of a spirit, usually as an apparition: the other is a residual haunting, essentially a playback of a past event, either visually or as sound. A residual haunting replays moments from the past regardless of whether a human audience is present or not.

How could this be so? One theory is that certain building materials — especially those used in older structures, like lead, slate and iron — possess qualities similar to the magnetic tape used in video and audio tape recorders.

It is interesting to note that extensive lead lining was used in the construction of Larnach Castle. According to experts who subscribe to this theory, when a traumatic event or period of high emotion occurs, these materials 'record' the moment for future 'replay'.

One of the world's most renowned residual hauntings is that of Anne Boleyn (1502–36), spotted haunting and oblivious to terrified witnesses in the very same section of the Tower of London where she was seen to wander just before being beheaded ...

During this time an uncooperative door continually unsettled Margaret Barker. Again and again she would close and lock it at night, only to find it open the next morning. Despite this, Margaret refuses to believe in ghosts, although she is the first to admit that her cynicism is a necessary security blanket: 'I have to be sceptical, don't I? I can't believe in ghosts — I have to live here!'

In 1982 the Barkers opened Larnach Castle to the public as an historic tourist attraction housing fascinating exhibits connected with the Larnach saga, and it has since become one of New Zealand's most identifiable buildings. And as tourists poured into its doors, ghostly stories of supernatural occurrences have poured out from visitors and staff alike.

One haunted hotspot appears to be Constance's boudoir, where Larnach's adulterous third wife was ensconced and, many speculate, the site of his cuckolding. It is accessed through plush, red velvet drapes and features an encased mannequin in the centre of the room sporting Constance's wedding gown. Many visitors have had peculiar experiences just outside these curtains, reporting an icy cold hand touching them on the nape of the neck. The superstition among staff is that these are the antics of Larnach's first wife, Eliza Jane, incensed that the bedroom of his unfaithful third wife, Constance, receives so much attention from visitors.

Several staff members clearing up after a function one night were spooked by the sound of heavy breathing emanating from the boudoir. It was clearly audible, even as they stood directly outside the drapes. A couple of them eventually plucked up enough courage to enter and found … nothing. Apart from the exhibits inside the room it was empty.

Lions and eagles guard the front stairwell to Larnach Castle, at times accompanied by the apparitions of William and Kate Larnach.

The breathing sound was never explained. Was it a residual haunting, an auditory replay of an event etched into the very fabric of the boudoir? The spirits of Constance and Douglas caught *in flagrante delicto*, perhaps? The staff members present can only speculate, and to those who were there that night, the sounds were frighteningly real. None of them have since entered this room as nonchalantly as they used to.

The sound of children giggling and whispering on the empty balconies is often heard by late-night staff working alone, and heavy footsteps have been heard on an isolated tower atop the castle. The only access to this tower is via a steeply winding turret, but after climbing the stairs to investigate, nothing out of the ordinary has ever been found. One evening, the current manager heard what sounded like the scraping of heavy furniture on the floor of the tower. Fearing theft, the manager rushed up the turret stairs and burst outside. Again, nothing was discovered within the confines of the parapet save the chilly night air and the strange feeling of a presence.

The castle's formidably grand entrance, with lions and eagles mounted either side of the stairwell, is where the apparitions of William and Kate have been reported by visitors. But staff member Deborah Rafills believes she had a close encounter with another spirit:

> I was showing a visiting Spanish travel writer around the castle and we were talking about what it would have been like living as a woman in a castle back in those days. And we got to talking about ghosts and I said if there is a ghost here it's probably Larnach's first wife, Eliza Jane, since she's the one who had the really hard life. Plus a lot of behaviour which she wouldn't have approved of went on in the castle after she died. … We were

laughing and joking about this as we headed down the front stairs and the next thing I felt someone push me hard from behind, right in the middle of the back. I fell down at least half a dozen steps and was quite badly hurt, what with a bleeding nose, a split lip and grazed knees. I was very upset. My suspicion is that it was Eliza Jane, who maybe didn't appreciate my laughing.

However, the space that inspires the most dread among staff members is the ballroom — the room Larnach never again entered after the death of his beloved daughter Kate. One of the features that disturbs people the most is the framed photographic portrait of Larnach on the wall at the far end of the ballroom. As viewers step back from the portrait, the features of the faded black and white photograph seem to coalesce into the grim visage of a skull. The further viewers retreat, the more profound the effect. Although just a trick of the eye, the effect is profoundly unsettling, especially when one remembers Larnach's macabre end.

Many visitors have reported witnessing an apparition inside the ballroom — the spectral figure of a woman in her twenties, matching the description of Kate and wearing a ball gown. A visiting psychic (who prefers to remain unnamed) claims to have encountered the presence of Larnach himself in the ballroom, which at that time was operating as a tea room. It is a mystery why the spirit of Larnach would choose to materialise in the one room he refused to enter in life:

When we went into the ballroom my mood changed instantly. I had no sooner sat down than a gruff old man came and stood beside me. He laid his hand on my shoulder, and I instantly became angry, as though his anger was transferring itself to me.

He was a morose, unhappy chap. I had the sense that he didn't
want to leave that which he had built. And that he was also
annoyed at the number of people passing through his space.

The ballroom was also the backdrop to the infamous night
in 1994 when the play *Larnach — Castle of Lies*, written by
Michaelanne Forster and produced by the Fortune Theatre
(see chapter 4), was staged. The script was based around
the final sad chapter of Larnach's life and a 'who's who' of
Dunedin was present for the one-off show. Outside it was a
mild and calm evening with no clouds or forecast of rain. At
the crucial point in the saga when Larnach holds the gun to
his head and fires, the heavens exploded as a terrible storm
whipped itself up seemingly out of nowhere; wind wailed
down the chimneys, causing fires to lick menacingly out of
fireplaces; hail thundered down on the roof of the castle so
heavily the actors' voices could not be heard above the bray;
doors mysteriously opened and slammed shut of their own
volition as temperatures turned arctic. Audience members
at first thought they were witnessing some very impressive
stage effects. Later on, when they learned this was not the
case, there was an extreme sense of unease all round.
Perhaps old Lanach's vanity prevailed even in death and he
wanted it known that he did not concur with his depiction in
the play …

One member of the audience that night was Sophie Barker,
daughter of Barry and Margaret Barker, who restored the
castle to its former glory. She grew up in Larnach Castle,
something she insists was no Cinderella fairytale:

I remember one experience I had when I was alone here during the witching hour. I was on the telephone when I felt and heard a presence come into the room and stand behind me. At first I thought it was my brother — I wasn't paying much attention because I was immersed in my phone conversation. Then the thought struck me. My brother wasn't at the castle that day. In fact I was all alone! I just dropped the phone and ran.

Sophie now runs the castle, but she adamantly refuses to live in it any more, or even stay overnight ...

There was obviously a darkness in the castle builder, and somehow the fruit of Larnach's labours seems forever cursed to be cloaked in that same darkness. William Larnach wanted to leave a legacy and he did — Larnach Castle, New Zealand's most renowned haunted site.

THE *GHOST HUNT* FILES

The *Ghost Hunt* team arrived at Larnach for their nocturnal investigation on a bright, sunny day that would eventually lead to an eventful night. Carolyn was excited about revisiting a place of which she had such fond memories from a childhood visit. But Brad was more cautious, and concerned about weather reports of a thick fog moving in, and of the effects that might have on the reliability of their surveillance equipment. Indeed the fog moved in rapidly just as darkness fell.

Walking around the top level, Carolyn was spooked by what she thought was the sound of a slamming door, and as she scurried downstairs to safety she came across a startling discovery: smeared handprints could clearly be seen on the outside of one of the many large windowpanes in Larnach's sizeable master bedroom. They appeared to have been clawing at the window. Carolyn brought Brad to the room to investigate, who confirmed that the handprints had not been there during the afternoon when he was in the room setting up cameras. He speculated that condensation from the fog may have brought them out, but was at a loss to explain how they got there. There is no balcony outside the window, which is two levels up, and the castle roof is many metres below. Carolyn succinctly summed it up: 'Who'd be trying to get into Larnach's bedroom? Larnach?! Or one of his three wives ...' She found her investigation experience terrifying, and so malevolent was the feeling emanating from the ballroom in particular, that Carolyn was barely able to take more than a few steps inside.

Michael, conversely, embarked on his investigation with great gusto. He had researched Larnach's life extensively and something about the cantankerous old bugger of a castle builder 'pushed his buttons'. Michael entered the castle walls that night on a pointed mission to goad the ghost of Larnach into putting in an appearance. Brad was bemused by Michael's strategy, but just as surprised by the results ...

Inside Larnach's study, Michael sat himself at the desk and issued a challenge to the spirit of the castle builder: 'Mr William Larnach, are you here? I call the ghost of William Larnach!' No sooner had Michael stood than he was beset by what he described later as 'a shiver over my spine and a rush of cold air whirling all around me and passing through me.' Shaken, Michael managed to click away a few photos in the room hoping to capture the presence on film. Disturbingly, one of Michael's shots revealed the blurred silhouette of a stocky man dressed in period garb, wearing a hat, standing ominously in the study doorway ...

Many visitors to Larnach Castle have either glimpsed or been menaced by this dark, stocky figure wearing period garb and hat that lurks in its corridors.

2. abandoned psychiatric hospital, near auckland

In the late 1990s, reforms in the field of mental health resulted in the closure of many of New Zealand's psychiatric hospitals. Some of these facilities have been demolished, others have been converted into institutions such as a college or museum, and a few lie empty awaiting redevelopment.

Whatever their incarnation, it is difficult to remove the stigma attached to these buildings or the negative energy that exists in them. Nearly every former psychiatric hospital is a reported haunt of the tortured souls of former inmates and staff members. The one remaining building from Seacliff Hospital in Dunedin, now a youth hostel, is renowned for its ghostly nocturnal visitors, while the abandoned site at Lake Alice has been used as the location for low-budget horror movies such as *The Waiting Place* (2001) and student films because of its highly charged atmosphere and terrifying ambience.

None, however, is more notorious than one particular abandoned psychiatric hospital located just outside one of the North Island's largest cities. Because the site may be redeveloped, and out of respect for those who suffered during its years of operation, we choose not to reveal the name or exact location of this facility. Needless to say its reputation as a haunted location precedes it, having many reliable ghost sightings reported both prior to and after its closure.

The hospital is situated on 60 hectares of grounds, once carefully tended but now ramshackle and overgrown. Entry is via a palm-lined avenue, flanked by villas, hospital buildings, a chapel and a football field. At the top of the driveway sits the imposing former administrative building. At the rear is the nurses' quarters, and on the opposite side of the complex, surrounded by hurricane wire, lies the maximum security wing. On the far right of the grounds, shrouded by trees, is the old morgue — the site of many autopsies ...

The first impression is of a sprawling, grand estate that has fallen into disrepair. Edge a little closer and the decay becomes overwhelming. Many of the buildings verge on the uninhabitable; ceilings are collapsing, paint is peeling and there is rubbish piled up in dark and dingy corridors. Broken windows, cobwebs and provocatively violent graffiti, sprayed in blood red, add to the atmosphere of desolation and terror.

For over half a century, the hospital's patients were considered social problems best kept under lock and key in the maximum security wing. The hospital itself was a veritable fortress.

This hospital was in operation from 1932 until 1999. Building began in 1929 when 20 patients from a nearby mental institution arrived at the site armed with 12 wheelbarrows and ten shovels. These poor, hapless patients were to build the foundations for their own future place of incarceration. By 1939 the hospital had eight wards, each with accommodation for 50 patients. By 1946 there was a total of 868 patients.

At that time, being mentally ill was considered a shameful secret and the inmates became social pariahs — the hospital was a virtual fortress. For over 60 years, it was known as a place to be feared, tainted by popular misconceptions about mental illness. With limited knowledge about psychiatric problems, all manner of patients were housed together — schizophrenics, manic-depressives, alcoholics, the criminally insane, even intellectually disabled children — and often subjected to inappropriate treatment.

This was the place where patients considered beyond rehabilitation were locked away for life. Razor-wire security fences and countless holding cells in the maximum security wing are testimony to this. However, some patients did attempt to escape. The owner of the café across the road still remembers the time an inmate, wearing a doctor's white coat, confused locals by diverting traffic at a junction before disappearing into the night. Another local recalls a group of escapees stealing earthmoving equipment to make a not-so-rapid getaway. Others recall the ringing of an alarm bell whenever a patient was on the run, warning residents of potential danger.

According to recent newspaper reports, some patients disappeared under more suspicious circumstances. In 1967 a teenage patient went missing, his death certificate stating 'death by drowning' in the nearby harbour. The day before he disappeared, however, he confided to his parents that the staff and other patients regularly beat him. His parents discovered he was covered in bruises and burns, and obviously terrified.

Another sad case is that of an 11-year-old boy who died in his hospital bed in 1968, reportedly of pneumonia. A fellow patient, however, later told a very different story, claiming that he had seen a male nurse kick the young boy in the back, and had even heard the crack as his back broke. The boy died the next morning.

One controversial treatment used in psychiatric hospitals in New Zealand and around the world at the time was ECT, or electroconvulsive therapy, whereby an electric current is passed through the brain for several seconds in an effort to disrupt or redirect 'faulty' behavioural impulses. A sad indictment of the misuse of this treatment occurred during the 1970s when one hospital was found to use ECT to punish children for trivial offences such as not making a bed or skipping dinner. Internationally renowned author Janet Frame was just one New Zealander who suffered repeated applications of ECT during her time at Christchurch's Sunnyside Hospital and Dunedin's Seacliff Hospital. In the authorised biography of her life, *Wrestling with the Angel: a Life of Janet Frame* by Michael King (Penguin, 2000), Frame talks of the traumatic procedure, and the memory loss and nightmares it triggered:

> *I dreamed waking and sleeping dreams more terrible than any I dreamed before ... [if] only I had been able to talk about some of the terror, I know I would not have so readily translated my feelings into action. It sounds silly, but my clothes haunted me ... everything tortures [me] and is on fire and is coloured.*

As in any hospital, there are always sad stories of misdiagnosis, tragedy and death. Obviously, there were many unhappy and ill people incarcerated here. Some died of natural causes, and others from drugs or physical abuse. Suicides also occurred here — the laundry allegedly a favoured location to commit this deed. Here, at least, patients were assured of relative privacy, and access to bed sheets or other useful items with which to end their lives.

With medical records unavailable to the public, it is impossible to estimate how many deaths occurred in this hospital during its years of operation. Needless to say it was a place of great sorrow, for even those who managed to survive lived here under great sufferance.

A spate of recent court cases has focused on mistreatment and abuse of patients in New Zealand's psychiatric institutions during the 1960s and 70s. More than 200 people have come forward to file complaints against the government,

The nurses' quarters are situated behind the administrative buildings. Life for staff at the hospital was equally oppressive and in the early days the nurses were practically institutionalised themselves.

recounting experiences of abuse, sexual assaults, beatings by staff and other patients, misuse of ECT, and drug injections as punishments. The results of these cases are still pending.

Even for staff, life at this hospital was difficult. In the early days, the nurses were practically institutionalised themselves — they lived, ate and worked here, with little respite from their job. Nurses were also expected to polish floors, clean windows, stoke boilers, work on the farm, deliver milk, maintain grounds and prepare meals for the patients in the absence of a cook. The work was hard, oppressive and underpaid. Nurses felt that they should have been able to care for their patients without compromising their time and energy on other jobs.

In 1968 the nurses at this hospital went on strike, working to rule. The hospital administration was forced to bring in unemployed people and volunteers to help around the hospital grounds and do the domestic chores. After just a week, the nurses had a victory, and nine other staff members were employed to look after the day-to-day running of the hospital.

Until this decision, male and female psychiatric nurses were also strictly segregated, not only in their living quarters but in the workplace as well. Strict segregation rules also applied to patients, and men were rarely seen on the female side of the complex, and vice versa.

The most common apparition seen at this hospital, and in hospitals all around the world, is that of a nurse. No one knows the identity of this tall, thin grey figure, known as the 'Grey Nurse', but the fact that she is generally seen in and around the nurses' home rather than in the wards indicates that she had a strong attachment to her former living quarters, whether in a positive or negative way.

Haunted hospitals

Nursing homes and hospitals are arguably the most haunted buildings of all. The most common apparition reported in hospitals across the globe is that of the 'Grey Nurse'. This tall, thin, transparent figure is often seen in wards hovering over patients in the dead of night, checking equipment and smoothing down beds. She has been known to prop patients up in their sleep (usually scaring them half to death in the process).

Paranormal experts believe that the Grey Nurse is a former staff member who had a traumatic experience during her working life. Perhaps she made a terrible medical error and took her life in remorse, or underwent a stressful situation that resulted in the loss of life. The Grey Nurse usually makes an appearance during times of crisis, perhaps as a harbinger of tragedy or to caution current staff members.

A classic of the nursing home ghost genre is the 'nurse in a blue-grey uniform', like that seen at the University College Hospital in London. It is said to be the spirit of a nurse who administered a lethal morphine dose to a patient and was so upset that she killed herself. Apparently this spirit only appears when screens go around a bed.

Another well-documented apparition made regular appearances at a maternity hospital, also in London. According to hospital lore, a nurse who was bottle-feeding an infant dozed off and smothered the baby as she slumped in her sleep. She was doomed to walk the wards for all eternity, tapping young nurses on the shoulder to keep them awake.

New Zealand's hospitals are riddled with tales of ghosts and lurking spirits. The old Waimate Hospital in Timaru was haunted by the spectre of the Grey Lady, said to be a patient who died during the 1960s. Apparently, this woman was beaten at home and afraid to leave the hospital for fear of further violence. It seems she never did ...

A Grey Lady haunts an old hospital in New Plymouth, while the former Dunedin Hospital (now the Stafford Gables Youth Hostel) is haunted by the apparition of two patients and a nurse. Guests have complained of being shaken in their beds in the middle of the night, possibly by the overzealous nurse spirit.

Security guards talk of hearing strange banging noises in the dead of night in the nurses' quarters, harking back to the tragic story of a cleaner who was crushed to death by her own floor-buffing machine. Others speak of lights flicking on and off in the middle of the night (the electricity has long been disconnected in most parts of the complex), while a guard tells of witnessing a transparent apparition floating silently between the wards one still summer evening.

Another former staff member, Yvonne, who currently lives on the edge of the premises looking after a group of troubled boys, recounts paranormal experiences that occurred during the years of operation and since its closure. She claims that the villa where the boys reside is haunted by the apparition of an elderly man who lurks in one of the bedrooms. She and other staff members have had strange encounters with ghostly figures in the laundry of that particular building.

On one occasion, Yvonne's five-year-old niece was visiting and drew some pictures of people she had seen coming from the horticultural area. One picture depicts nurses, dressed in uniforms with crosses helping a patient in a wheelchair. The other shows patients in gowns walking through a grove of trees. The little girl told her aunt that these were 'the nurses bringing the people up' and not to worry, because 'they can't come inside anyway, they're not allowed to'. Yvonne believes her niece witnessed the apparition of former nurses and patients at the hospital.

Because of its enormous scale and bleak outlook, this particular abandoned hospital has been used as a location for horror movies and music videos with a dark theme. During the filming of a big-budget international vampire movie in 2004, crew members claimed that they were being grabbed from behind by cold, clammy disembodied hands and terrorised in certain rooms. Before filming commenced, the production called in a Maori kaumatua, or elder, to bless the premises and to clear it of its evil spirits. According to the kaumatua, 'there is no getting rid of the ghosts of this place'. He claimed that the hospital was riddled with the sadness of the past, and that all he could do was appease the spirits sufficiently for the filming to continue.

Two other local filmmakers experienced an inexplicable event during a location survey of the premises, and captured it all on film. As they entered a room at the end of a long corridor, a spittoon beside a dentist's chair — long disconnected from an electrical source — began to gurgle, rattle and groan on its own. 'It was unplugged, and then suddenly when we were filming around it, it just turned on and started gurgling,' said Luke, one of the still incredulous filmmakers. Perhaps this was a sinister warning for the filmmakers to keep their distance, and leave the spirits of this abandoned hospital in peace?

THE *GHOST HUNT* FILES

Of all the locations investigated by the *Ghost Hunt* team, this one had the most menace. The scale of the complex and the distance between buildings is imposing enough, but add to this the state of disrepair, the lack of comforts, the emptiness and the terrifying stories, and you have one extremely scary location!

While the whole complex is said to be haunted, the focus for our investigation was on two of the larger buildings — the maximum security wing and the nurses' quarters. Carolyn felt she had drawn the short straw being given maximum security; but in fact, the nurses' quarters is an epicentre of paranormal activity, with many reported sightings of an apparition known as the Grey Nurse.

A photograph taken by a building inspector during a routine examination of the building in 2004 shows a wispy figure lurking in a window, one storey above ground level. Could this be the shady spectre of a nurse who refuses to leave her former place of employment?

Wandering through the ground level of the nurses' home, Michael sensed a distinct drop in temperature as he entered

The nurses' quarters is an epicentre of paranormal activity — this wispy figure photographed in 2004 is reputed to be the Grey Nurse that haunts the building.

one of the tiny bedrooms. He felt a strange presence in the room, as if something terrible had happened there. The evidence captured on Brad's cameras backed up Michael's emotions. As Michael entered the room, little balls of light appeared on some wooden planks stacked up in the corner of the room. These lights were determined not to be reflections from Michael's helmet light or his torch, nor were they reflections from the window, but instead moved consistently in a pattern. According to Brad, these lights appear to be using Michael's own energy, which is how a spirit, usually in an early incarnation, manifests itself. These lights are also referred to as orbs, a physical manifestation of residual energy.

Carolyn had a similarly unusual experience in the maximum security wing. It occurred upstairs near the holding cells, an area of great psychic energy. Carolyn described seeing waving lights, measuring from the 'floor to my height, in rainbow colours, sort of like a prism of light when it's been raining'. As she was seeing these colours, the footage from her helmet camera detected an anomalous light frequency shift from red to green to yellow.

This can, of course, occur in any camera equipment under low-light conditions – the camera may just be trying to adjust from black and white to colour, reacting to a light source. Whatever the physical reason for the interference, there is no way that Carolyn could have known about the frequency shift as it all happens internally on the camera and tape and there is no other logical explanation for it. This strange occurrence also begs the question, Where was the light source causing the camera to adjust itself? In the pitch black of the maximum security wing, there were no internal or external light sources. Was this a paranormal incident?

Infra-red non-contact thermometers

It is a fact that energy must be present in order to alter temperature — air cannot become hotter or colder unless something is affecting it in some way or another. Paranormal experts believe that ghosts absorb energy, whether heat, light or emotional, causing the area around the entity to be several degrees cooler. While most perceptive ghost hunters can physically sense a temperature drop, a thermometer is a useful tool used to verify the existence of a cold spot.

The thermometers used in *Ghost Hunt* are handheld devices that use an infra-red laser beam (accurate to 30 metres) to record temperatures. The thermometer provides a digital readout capable of being read in the dark.

Of all the areas in and around maximum security, Carolyn found the cells the most oppressive, accompanied by a feeling of 'absolute horror'. She likewise bid a hasty retreat from the bathroom after Brad sent her in to check a temperature reading. After confirming that the room was freezing, she took a photograph of the shower stalls that she felt housed a strange presence. What that photograph would reveal justified Carolyn's trepidation. Peering out from behind a shower stall is what appears to be an eye surrounded by bone structure. It is a disturbing image, and one intensified by the history of criminally insane patients and inhumane medical treatments ...

EMF meters

One of the most useful tools in any ghost hunt is an EMF (electromagnetic field) meter or trifield meter. This instrument detects fluctuations in magnetic, microwave and radioactive waves. These rays surround and permeate all of physical reality, and include X-rays, light, radio waves, and ultraviolet rays. Televisions, light bulbs, microwave ovens and computers all give off electromagnetic waves, as do human beings and animals. EMF's are also created by weather in outer space such as geomagnetic storms and solar flares.

An EMF meter is a useful device for ghost hunters as it indicates whether there is an unexpected source of energy — or in other words, a ghostly presence! Researchers believe that ghosts are electromagnetic in origin, either giving off their own energy or drawing energy from the atmosphere around them. Therefore, erratic fluctuations in EMF may indicate spiritual activity in a location. An electromagnetic reading of 7 mG (milligauss) is generally accepted as the level indicating a supernatural presence.

Another theory is that human consciousness is made up of energy — in other words, we are animated by electricity. As Einstein discovered, energy cannot be created or destroyed; it can only be changed from one form of energy to another. So the theory goes, the electrical impulse transmitted through the nervous system is not destroyed on death; it is merely transformed. If this is true, then it is feasible that our consciousness, or what we call our spirit or our soul, survives the death of the body.

The Trifield meter used on *Ghost Hunt* is a state-of-the-art device designed for natural field measurements in specialised research areas. It has been designed to ignore the AC fields of power lines and appliances, and therefore is more accurate than lesser EMFs. The device has an alarm that will sound when levels go above an acceptable level. When a positive EMF reading occurs, it is advisable to take as many photographs as possible and to check for temperature changes. While none of these tools can alone prove the existence of ghosts, they all work together in paranormal research.

However, the night was only to get worse for Carolyn, as an extreme reading on the trifield meter triggered Brad's computer alarm and she was sent to the morgue to investigate. Could there be a worse place for anyone to go in the dead of night?

As Carolyn entered the morgue, which is a tiny, cell-like building hidden behind a grove of trees, she sensed immediately the death and decay of the past. The building itself still smelt strongly of blood and formaldehyde. Unfortunately, the communication link between Brad and Carolyn failed as soon as she entered the morgue, and with no external support she bid a hasty retreat without checking the reading of the meter — conveniently placed in the fridge where the bodies of the deceased were stored — and without taking a photograph. We can therefore only speculate about what specifically caused the EMF alarm to sound in this awful, scary place ...

Digital ghost photography

The beauty of a digital camera is that the results are instant — you don't have to wait for developing to see the fruits of your labour. They also provide an inexpensive alternative to 35 mm photography, freeing the ghost photographer to snap randomly without worrying about exorbitant developing costs. Using digital photography, there are fewer chances of anomalies caused by flawed film stock or double exposures.

Of course, there are some problems associated with taking so-called 'ghost photographs' on a digital camera. Some of the earliest, low-end digital cameras were made with imaging chips that would create visual 'noise' or distortion under low-light conditions. The resultant images were regularly littered with spots that appeared white or light-coloured where pixels had not been filled in. Over-enthusiastic ghost hunters claimed these flaws to be orbs, whereas many images were proved to have no paranormal foundation at all. Other false orb images are caused by light refracting off the camera lens. This occurs when the camera flash bounces off a reflective surface, causing a perfectly round ball of light that appears to hover in mid-air. These balls of light can also be created by an external light source.

To determine whether a photograph of an orb is genuine or not, it is advisable to take as many photographs in one location as possible. If orbs appear in exactly the same place in consecutive photographs, chances are it is a refracted lens or a spot on the camera glass.

But if the orbs appear to be moving, as seen in a sequence of photos, or in a pattern, it may constitute evidence of paranormal phenomena.

3. waitomo caves hotel

The Waitomo Caves Hotel is an historic, expansively grand building perched on a steep, bush-secluded limestone hill in the Waitomo region of the North Island. Its long, winding driveway meanders through a tall stand of trees until the last bend reveals a majestic view of the hotel frontage — a charming hotchpotch of varied architectural styles.

The hotel is a popular spot for travellers exploring the extensive tourist cave systems of Waitomo and, as New Zealand's self-proclaimed 'most haunted hotel', it has become

Almost a century since it first opened as a government-built hostel, Waitomo Caves Hotel's majestic frontage is made of many different architectural styles.

a popular destination for psychics, paranormal pundits and film crews from all over the world. Bathtubs drip blood, and an ancient Maori princess stalks the hallways where doors are seen to open and close on their own. On any ghost-hunting map, this place is a must-see. Supernatural tales have attached themselves like glow-worms to this atmospheric hotel ever since it opened (on a less imposing scale) in 1910 as a government-run hostel built to accommodate the growth industry of tourism in the area.

Prior to that the Waitomo region was known as one of the most inhospitable parts of New Zealand owing to its rugged geography. Beneath its hilly surface lies a labyrinth of intertwined caves. Many of these are regarded by Maori as tapu, and inhabited by taniwha and patupaiarehe (see chapter 6). The cave system was known for years, but with the discovery in 1887 of the now-legendary glow-worm caves by Maori chief Tane Tinorau and English surveyor Fred Mace, curious sightseers started trekking to the area in droves.

Concerted efforts were made to tame the land into a visitor-friendly place. Roads were constructed, and wild pigs driven from the forest. In these early days, cave-tourism was rather crude. Guides would show visitors around by candlelight and, after slipping and sliding on the soft, wet surface, parties would emerge with shoes and hemlines caked in clay. In his book *A History of Waitomo* (1983), writer Vaughan Morgan recalls his aunt being lowered down into the caves by a rope tied around her waist.

The government hostel was a welcome addition to the tourist trade but soon found itself unable to cope with the growing number of visitors to the area. In 1928 extensions were added to the original central European-style building — a concrete wing was added, with Cape Dutch-style pillars and facades, and Spanish missionary-style decks and patios. As well as extra rooms, the new interior contained a large dining room designed in the popular art deco style of the day, in addition to a kitchen and servants' quarters. And so the eccentrically impressive Waitomo Caves Hotel, as we know it today, emerged ... and chilling, ghostly tales started to flow forth from visitors and staff alike.

Why this is the case is not certain. It may have to do with the fact that deep beneath the hill on which the hotel is built there are tapu, spirit-infested caves. Until the advent of modern tourism, the cave systems were used to bury the dead. Legend has it that chief Tane Tinorau of Kawhia was buried in a recess over the entrance of nearby Ruakuri Cave, and skeletal remains of adults and children have been found in caverns above that particular spot.

Another possibility for the high level of paranormal activity may be the region's bloody past. The history of Maori occupation goes back to 1350, and two fearsome battles are known to have been fought in the area involving three or four sub-tribes to whom Waitomo was home. Battles also raged here between Kingite Maori and the British army. According to other local sources, the hotel is actually built on the site of a Maori pa.

Or perhaps the haunting of Waitomo Caves Hotel is linked to tragedies that happened inside the hotel itself. At least two tragic deaths are alleged to have occurred on its grounds. The restaurant is said to exhibit high levels of spiritual activity, and inexplicable cold spots are often reported in the hotel's ballroom, where local dances were once held. The spectral

Haunted hotels in New Zealand

There are many hotels in New Zealand said to be haunted, most of them historic boutique hotels with long, colourful histories. Unlike the Waitomo Caves Hotel, which proudly embraces its ghostly ambience, many of these establishments speak about their resident spooks in hushed tones and downplay their existence entirely.

The magnificent Chateau, for instance, which perches on the lower slopes of Mt Ruapehu, is haunted by a ghost called Charlie who hanged himself from the plumbing when the building operated as a psychiatric hospital during the 1940s. Legend has it that Charlie still haunts Room 305. While this story is widely known, the Chateau downplays any talk of ghostly entities, fearing that the stigma will scare off particularly superstitious guests.

Another allegedly haunted hotel is the Skotel Alpine Resort in Whakapapa Village, near Mt Ruapehu. This building was also used as a mental institution in the early twentieth century, and is said to boast two ghosts — one a mean-spirited doctor, the other a friendly entity who does no harm.

One establishment that is happy to talk about its resident ghost is Princes Gate Hotel in Rotorua. This is not the original location for this beautiful, grand building — it was built in Waihi in 1897, but was dismantled and transported piece by piece to Rotorua by rail in 1917. The hotel's reconstruction in its current position began in 1921. According to its owners, the hotel still holds energies from its past life. In particular, Room 29 is haunted by a female spirit who only ever appears to male guests. Some customers have refused to return to the

The apparition of a beautifully dressed woman is the spirit in residence of Room 29 at Princes Gate Hotel, Rotorua. She appears to male guests.

room after being subjected to her night-time visitations. Entertainer Sir Howard Morrison reported that a friend of his staying in Room 29 beheld the apparition of a beautifully dressed woman at the window. His face as white as a ghost, he quickly arrived at Sir Howard's door, just down the corridor, to tell the tale.

The Racecourse Hotel in Riccarton in Christchurch is allegedly haunted by the restless soul of its former manager, David Fraser. A violent man who died a violent death, Fraser was murdered by an unknown assailant in his upstairs bedroom. Apparently, his ghost still wanders the corridors of the hotel searching for his murderer.

sounds of laughter, chatter and piano music are often heard emanating from within its walls. Is it possible that, in its heyday, the hotel was such an integral part of community life that the spirits of the departed simply gravitated back there in the afterlife?

Martin Sandifer is the manager and co-owner of Waitomo Caves Hotel. He is a delightful and amiable raconteur, and the journey to the hotel is worth it just to meet Martin and be regaled by his wonderful stories. As the last to lock up each night, he has had his fair share of spooky encounters, commonly doors opening in front of or closing behind him of their own accord. Phantom footsteps in the upstairs corridors occur virtually every night, as do other strange, inexplicable noises and flickering lights. On one memorable occasion the front-of-house floodlights turned on of their own volition at 3 a.m. These lights were not connected to a sensor or timer, and Martin activated them manually in the early evening and switched them off after the last guests had retired. He investigated the padlocked console where the switch was housed and found no sign that it had been tampered with. Martin has since become so inured to such strange goings-on that he accepts these things as part of the mystery of the hotel. One of the place's most fascinating mysteries, as he tells it, involves the spirit of a Maori princess:

> This story was originally told to me by an old Maori. I had the facts verified and they all turned out to be true. A British regiment was camped in the valley below this hill – where the main road of the village is now. And this hill was actually a pa. One of the chief's daughters became enamoured of a British soldier, and of a night she would creep down through the bushes

on the side of the hill so they could meet. One misty night, as
she was sneaking out to meet her paramour, she was sighted by
a sentry. The sentry mistook her for a warrior, and, thinking an
attack was imminent, he shot her.

The spirit of the Maori princess haunts the wing of the hotel housing the honeymoon suite – fitting considering the 'star-crossed lovers' aspect to her sad demise. Over the decades the princess has frequently been seen by visitors staying in the suite, usually observed staring sorrowfully out of the window. But other accounts have emerged from the suite: of guests feeling their bed clothing being removed; of an indentation of a human form appearing on the bed; some have merely felt a presence in the room; others have heard an overhead light bulb ticking even when the power is turned off. This spirit is also said to have taken residence in a particular hotel attic, and her mournful moaning can often be heard wafting out of this area. She allegedly emerges to spend her nights restlessly searching for her long lost lover, drifting through the upstairs hallways where staff members have encountered her apparition.

In an odd twist of fate, this ghost (according to Martin) may have been inadvertently responsible for the creation of another. Even odder, the origin of the story is centred in Room 14, the room where Elizabeth II stayed when visiting the Waitomo Caves in 1950. The actual year the awful event transpired is not clear, but is said to have been shortly after the royal visit. As the story goes, a young male guest at the hotel was terrified to feel the presence of a spirit pass through his body in an upstairs hallway. The location of this occurrence suggests that it was the spirit of the Maori princess. Either way, the shattering encounter with the otherworldly was too much for the poor fellow to bear. After heading down to the bar for a stiff drink and passing his terrifying tale on to other patrons, he duly returned to Room 14 and committed suicide. His ghost now haunts the upstairs hallways as well – a pale death mask is sometimes glimpsed in a window reflection sporting a hideous expression of horror.

Hanging is generally accepted to have been the poor chap's chosen mode of suicide, but an incident in Room 14's bathroom has raised suggestions that he may have slit his wrists in the bathtub. Some years after the suicide, a cleaning lady entered the bathroom only to see the tub awash and dripping with blood. Concerned, she contacted the manager at the time and went to fetch some cleaning products. On her return the bathtub was found shiny and clean.

Martin contends that the hotel's ground level houses yet another tragic spirit, supposedly that of a young boy, a victim of a misfortune that purportedly occurred in the 1930s. According to the tale, an unmarried servant girl would smuggle her young son at night into the servants' quarters, which were a cluster of tiny rooms off a long corridor nicknamed 'Cat Alley'. She endeavoured to keep his existence a secret from hotel management. One night, as the young boy was skipping through the kitchen immediately adjacent to 'Cat Alley', he knocked over a huge pot of boiling water which landed directly on top of him. He reportedly died of third-degree burns.

The apparition of a boy has been witnessed by kitchen staff running through 'Cat Alley', the kitchen, and more commonly, the restaurant. It seems this young spirit prefers to reveal himself to other children. One former staff member, Dania, says her young son hated being in the hotel and he complained about a strange little boy who always followed him around in the restaurant. Indeed, the ghostly sound of childish giggling can often be heard in this area, but when staff investigate no source for the laughter is ever found. Staff members have taken to calling this playful spirit Daniel.

The restaurant appears to be a real hotbed of paranormal activity. Some staff (and even the occasional visiting psychic)

The white, misty blur (top right) hovering close to the entrance to the hotel resembles the supernatural vapour ectoplasm.

say that walking into the empty dining room often feels like walking into a room full of people, as though its walls are alive with the spirits of the past. In a nook to one end of the restaurant there is a cosy art deco bar. One night, as a bar patron was loudly declaring that he did not believe in ghosts, the glass he was holding in his hand spontaneously shattered. He retired to his room somewhat sheepishly soon after and, although unharmed by the incident, his sceptical stance was solidly shaken ...

Two further guest rooms upstairs are worthy of note. Debra Crozier, a Canadian guest staying in room 12-A, accidentally spilt talcum powder on the floor. She turned around to look for something to clean it up and when she turned back, a footprint had mysteriously appeared in the powder. She held her foot above it, for comparison, but discovered that her own was much too large — the footprint appeared to be the size of a child's.

Dr Pamela Heath, an esteemed American paranormal expert staying in this same room at another time, observed her door repeatedly opening and closing. On asking the spirit to stop, she claims that it did. Dr Heath then brought along some professional ghost-hunting equipment, including a trifield meter, which elicited an electromagnetic flux reading outside the door to 12-A well above 7 mG. She concluded that this indicated a high level of spiritual activity, and she personally authenticated Waitomo Caves Hotel's standing as a haunted site.

Room 25, also known as the Family Room, is another source of unusual activity — so much so that many staff refuse to enter it. Shower curtains mysteriously open and close, and many guests find their personal items are moved from place to place. One staff member reported standing in the entrance to the room and viewing a shadowy figure disappear through a wall further down the corridor.

In addition, an infamous photograph of the Waitomo Caves Hotel was taken in broad daylight by a guest in Room 25 (see page 57). The angle shows the front of the hotel and an Asian couple in the opposite wing, standing on their balcony which coincidentally extends from room 12-A. They are pointing at a white, misty swirl hovering in the air above the entrance to the hotel — a swirl that resembles ectoplasm, which is a supernatural vapour sometimes found in the presence of spiritual activity ...

THE *GHOST HUNT* FILES

As the *Ghost Hunt* trio ascended the drive to the hotel, Michael commented on its similarity, in both style and setting, to Oregon's Timberline Lodge, which doubled for the spooky Overlook Hotel in the supernatural thriller *The Shining*. A little ill at ease with the comparison, the others had to agree. Team leader Brad briefed the other two ghost hunters and photographic evidence was examined, including the shot of the Asian couple and ectoplasm as well as an eerie photo taken in the hotel that portrays a 'melting' corridor. The photographer who snapped it reported feeling as though he was being dragged back in time. Brad also warned the others of the hotel's eccentric layout — because of its higgledy-piggledy construction history, some floor plans did not accord

The photographer reported a feeling of being dragged through time while in this hotel corridor.

with the current structure and the end result resembles a maze. No two rooms were the same, the floors generally crooked. Losing one's way during the nocturnal investigations would not be outside the realms of possibility.

Michael was booked into the Honeymoon Suite for the night, and Carolyn into Room 25, the Family Room. Hotel staff member Selena led Carolyn to her room, giving her intimate knowledge of why the haunted hotel's workers tended to feel so on edge in the place. Selena related first-hand tales of doors that opened and closed of their own accord, and, on reaching Room 25, proved too timid to enter. Carolyn was not feeling reassured, and even less so when the lock on the door at first refused to allow her admittance.

Vortex

A vortex is described as a spiralling vertical column of bright light, normally white, but when more intense levels of spiritual energy are present appearing red, blue or green. The vortex is said to be a portal through which ghosts pass from the spiritual realm to the earthly world, whereon they manifest themselves either as orbs or as apparitions. Vortices are rarely caught on photograph, but when they do, provide a chillingly spectacular image.

A vortex — the gateway between the spirit and physical worlds — manifesting in the ballroom of the Waitomo Caves Hotel.

Night descended, and with surveillance equipment set up and ready to go the ghost hunt began. Carolyn handled the lower floors and Michael the upper levels. Michael had just stepped off the first floor landing when the phenomenon of which both Martin and Selena had spoken occurred — a double door closed behind him after he walked through it. Michael investigated but could find no technical reason for the door's mysterious behaviour. Michael then investigated Room 12-A and Room 14 but encountered no spiritual activity. However, on a landing beneath the Honeymoon Suite he sensed a strange presence, prompting him to click away with his camera.

Carolyn found her search of the lower level to be disturbing, and she was on edge the whole time. In the ballroom she reported to Brad via two-way radio that she was seeing strange colours in the periphery of her vision — a phenomenon Carolyn is prone to, and indicating a gift for aura sensitivity. Brad advised her to take photos, and two of these photos, when analysed later, revealed intensely green-coloured manifestations to one side of the ballroom, roughly the height and size of a young child. Brad contended that these were photographs of a vortex, a portal through which a ghost travels from the spirit world to manifest itself in our world.

Carolyn was still inside the hotel's ballroom when Brad, still in the van parked to one side of the hotel entrance, spotted a moving orb on the surveillance cameras. It appeared to be floating freely, clearly visible above the front steps. He asked Carolyn to come out and investigate, and as she emerged through the hotel's front door, the orb started to dance playfully around her. Carolyn could not see it with her naked

The residual haunting of a 1950s suicide known to lurk in the upstairs corridor appears with a grotesque death mask.

eye, and neither could Brad, though it was plainly visible on the surveillance system — a ball of spiritual energy that interacted with our erstwhile ghost hunter. Eventually, the ball of light drifted off into the murky darkness.

Brad extensively analysed the footage but could arrive at no conclusion other than that the team had managed to catch a moving orb on camera. Taking into account the series of paranormal events, he conjectured that the green vortex photographed in the ballroom may have been the spirit of the little boy who died in the kitchen. The orb may have been Daniel's residual spiritual energy, not yet formed into a fully fledged apparition, following Carolyn around. Already agape from their evening's harrowing adventures, the other two were quick to agree that this sounded eminently plausible.

By this point, anything seemed possible at the Waitomo Caves Hotel.

Yet one more shock was yet to come from the analysis. When Brad examined Michael's photographs, taken from the landing beneath the Honeymoon Suite, he spotted another disturbing anomaly in a photo of an old six-panel window. Five panes of glass reveal nothing but the darkness of the night outside. But, when enlarged, the glass panel in the upper left corner reveals what appears to be a horrifyingly grotesque death mask. The face looks decayed, the bloated tongue hangs out of the mouth and the head hangs limply from the neck. Michael had taken this photograph with a sensation of discomfiture, as though sensing a presence somewhere nearby. Had the apparition of the nameless suicide victim, a residual haunting caught eternally in its death-moment, been hovering behind him as he snapped the photo?

Larnach Castle (see chapter 1) stands as a silent sentinel on the outskirts of Dunedin. The family that originally occupied the castle has a dark and potent history of murder, illness, suicide and adultery.

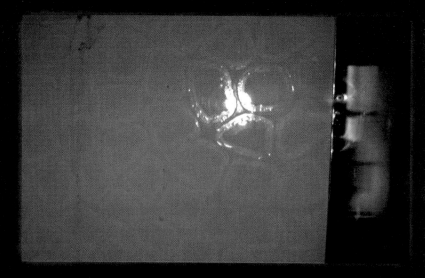

A phantom, bearing a facial bone structure and baleful stare, was photographed in a shower stall at an abandoned psychiatric hospital near Auckland (see chapter 2).

This aura of bright colour appearing inexplicably in the middle of the ballroom at the Waitomo Caves Hotel (see chapter 3) is thought to be a vortex, a portal through which spirits travel to manifest in the physical world.

A gruesome image, manifesting as a grotesque death mask and perhaps the result of a residual haunting, captured on film at the window of the Honeymoon Suite at Waitomo Caves Hotel.

Ghost Hunt *investigator Carolyn Taylor sporting the helmet-camera that vividly recorded both her paranormal encounters and her reaction to them.*

Brad Hills directs the Ghost Hunt investigators and manages the surveillance cameras, motion detectors, computers, EMF meters and other ghost-detection gadgets.

A ghostly figure (centre) can be discerned gliding through the walls of Dunedin's Fortune Theatre (see chapter 4), one of several spectral phenomena found at the former church.

Stately Riccarton House (see chapter 5) conceals a tragic love story — is this apparition seen on an upstairs balcony the ghost of original owner Jane Deans, another paranormal entity, or something else?

In the area around Whatipu Lodge (see chapter 6), the levels of spiritual activity are intense — this cluster of orbs was one of several recorded on camera during the Ghost Hunt investigation

Matilda Gibbons, one of the family members who lived in Whatipu Lodge when it was first built in 1860, is rumoured to be the Pink Lady who haunts its halls (see chapter 6).

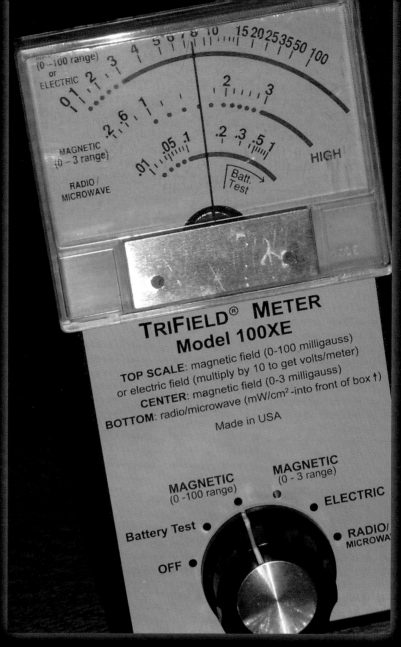

A trifield meter detects fluctuations in magnetic, microwave and radioactive waves — a useful device for ghost hunters as it can indicate sources of paranormal energy.

4. the fortune theatre, dunedin

A small regional theatre company cosily ensconced in a charming old church — it sounds rather calm and serene. Surely not a typical backdrop for terrifying tales of haunting? Yet the Fortune Theatre is infamous as *the* most haunted site in what is generally regarded New Zealand's most haunted city, Dunedin. And it would seem the restless spirits of churchgoers from days gone by might not be exactly thrilled at the fate of their beloved place of worship ...

The Trinity Methodist Church, within whose walls the Fortune Theatre Company now resides, was built in 1869. Designed by renowned Dunedin architect R.A. Lawson, its neo-Gothic bluestone façade was considered a perfectly desirable addition to the city's streetscape.

The original minister of the church, however, was a character who created a few ripples in the fabric of his congregation. As well as being a man of the cloth, Alfred Robertson Fitchett was a teacher and scholar. He held the Chair of Classics at Dunedin's Selwyn College for 20 years, and regularly wrote editorial for the *Otago Daily Times*. His liberal views often earned him the enmity of his starchy and conservative parishioners. One paper he published in 1876, supporting Darwin's Theory of Evolution and arguing against a literal interpretation of the Book of Genesis, caused considerable stir across the city. Fitchett finally resigned and moved on from his thorny congregation in 1879 — the next minister was more to the liking of the worshippers.

On Christmas Day 1977 the congregation held its last service on the site, before amalgamating with the Central Methodist Mission 50 metres down the road. The Fortune Theatre Company, one of very few professional regional theatre companies in New Zealand, moved into the space shortly after. The players had been searching for suitable permanent premises since forming in 1974, and the church building seemed a perfect fit. The curious split-level design allowed the construction of a main stage on the upper level and a smaller more intimate stage underneath. But soon after taking residence actors and technicians (and audience members) started reporting strange experiences, and eerie stories of the supernatural began to resound from its walls.

Tales spread of sinister voices hissing lines offstage, and of well-secured lights tumbling from the lighting grid. There were also numerous reports of a phantom audience member — a theatregoer would turn to converse with a man in old-fashioned garb sitting beside them, who would give no response. When the theatregoer turned again, the figure would have mysteriously vanished, as though never there in the first place.

It is debatable that theatre people are dramatic by nature, not to mention soaked in the superstitions of the stage, and theatres that do not claim to house a resident ghost are few and far between, but reports kept coming, from a variety of reliable sources, until the haunting of the Fortune Theatre became firmly etched in local folklore. Interestingly, whereas hauntings in general are accompanied by a tale of a tragic or gruesome demise, no such story seems connected to the Fortune.

One notion among members of the theatre company is that the ghost is the spirit of an angry parishioner, incensed that their former place of worship has been overtaken by a liberal-minded, free-thinking bunch of bohemian thespians, plying their craft on once holy boards. Andrew Smith, owner-operator of *Hair Raiser Ghost Walk Tours,* a tour company specialising in excursions through Dunedin's haunted hotspots, is well-versed in local ghost lore and subscribes wholeheartedly to the angry parishioner theory:

> *My belief is that the original parishioners of the church are unhappy with the transformation of their building. And their ghosts are still here, causing disturbances. Many people claim to have heard voices, and that strange feeling that someone's watching you. You turn around, there's no one there. I myself have seen a mysterious shadow in the building. It was lurking on the left-hand side of the stage. The people I've spoken to say that the strangest things start happening when the more risqué plays are being staged. And there have even been injuries to actors performing in them.*

A quick glance through the bills of the theatre's past performances demonstrates a plethora of productions that are not recommended for the prudish, including obscure and cult classics such as *Well Hung* (unpublished; first performed 1974), *Foreskin's Lament* (1981), *The Sex Fiend* (unpublished; first performed 1989) and *Conjugal Rites* (1990); explicitly gay-themed plays *The Killing of Sister George* (1965) and *Fortune and Men's Eyes* (1967); as well as David Mamet's drama about sexual harassment, *Oleanna* (1992) and David Williamson's *The Removalists* (1972), both controversial at the time. *Strippers* (1985) almost made it to opening night but was ultimately vetoed by disapproving female production staff and cancelled under threats of industrial action. Ironically enough, a couple of hit plays about male strippers — *Ladies Night* (unpublished; first performed 1988) and *Ladies Night II* (unpublished; first performed 1993) — are credited with turning the Fortune's financial fortunes around in the early nineties. Either way, it is a list saucy enough to send any god-fearing Victorian-era churchgoer spinning in their grave.

Andrew Smith has many spooky yarns to tell about his hometown's ghosts. He even has a theory as to why Dunedin (and the Fortune in particular) suffers such high levels of spiritual activity:

> A subterranean spring is situated beneath the site of what was Dunedin's first cemetery. And its tributaries flow beneath the city. There was a lot of controversy when the cemetery was relocated and the bodies disinterred. And there is a legend that not all of the bodies were actually moved to the new site. It is said that some were just dumped under a large mound, which can still be seen there today. Because of this, many people believe that the water from the spring is cursed, and that this 'spirit water' flows under Dunedin. It's curious to note that if you follow the course of the tributaries, they flow beneath many of Dunedin's haunted sites, most notably the Fortune Theatre.

Haunted spring water carrying the spirits of the dead may strike some as far-fetched, but so far no alternative explanation has been forthcoming as to what has got Dunedin in general, and the denizens of the Fortune in particular, so spooked.

Fortune lighting technician Corey Anderson knows only too well the sense of dread the theatre can induce. From his lighting box high above the main stage, he related one of his more chilling paranormal encounters:

I was all alone setting up on stage one day when I glimpsed a person over my shoulder, on the edge of the stage. They looked like they were reading through some lines, as an actor would, but I knew no cast members were around at the time. I turned the stage lights on, and suddenly they were gone. It was bizarre.

Corey has also felt inexplicably cold presences in the lighting box itself, normally lurking over his shoulder and seeming so real that he has been distracted enough to miss vital lighting cues during some performances:

I believe the thing with ghosts and theatres is this: actors think they have something to prove. That's why they become actors. And I think in many ways that attitude seeps over to theatre technicians as well. And a theatre ghost will unplug a light, blow a bulb or somehow manage to ruin some cue you've carefully orchestrated. And they do it to remind you that you're not meant to be playing god. You're just here to put on a show. I think they're just trying to keep you on your toes and keep you honest.

Chris Hendry's young daughters are actors and have appeared on stage in various productions at the Fortune. She says they would both insist she walk them to their change rooms when they arrived, and pick them up from there once they had completed their performances:

I was never allowed to wait out in the car, because they were too spooked to enter the theatre alone. And I don't blame them. One of my daughters had a change room at the far end of a downstairs corridor. And there was always a strange chill — just to one side of the corridor. One side was always room temperature, the other side freezing. And there was this feeling of a presence, and always the sensation of someone or something watching you. So much so that you'd always be spinning around to check.

Chris' theory as to why spirits love theatres so much correlates with Corey's:

Actors get on stage and mess with people's lives, and present them in different ways. And often the characters are based on real people. And I think the spirits are just moving around and keeping check on them.

Yule Guttenbeil, who runs the Fortune's box office, is usually the first to open the doors and the last to lock up and leave. He has had two disconcerting experiences, both involving apparitions of children:

I was opening up one weekend and was heading through the bar to the box office as I always do. As I walked through the bar I noticed a young boy sitting in the corner. At first I thought nothing of it. It's not unusual to have people sitting around any part of a theatre. So I walked right past him. Then the realisation struck me. The theatre was closed, and I'd just opened it. It should have been empty. I turned back around, but he'd disappeared. I knew straight away it was a ghost. There have been ghost stories around this place for so long that I just accepted it.

Yule's second encounter occurred one evening after a rehearsal:

> *I heard a strange noise in the theatre, just adjacent to the box office, and went to check if anyone was around. I entered the theatre and the stage lights were still on and it looked empty. Then I looked up to the back corner of the audience seating, near where the soundman usually sits. And I saw a young girl in white. Just standing there. Not moving. I called out and she didn't respond. I started heading up the steps, to find out what she was doing there. But before I was even halfway she just seemed to vanish.*

Adding weight to Yule's claim is a photograph taken recently in the Fortune's foyer. It is angled through double glass doors and towards the box office. In the background is a beautiful Gothic leadlight window. Yet beneath the window, appearing to float in mid-air, is the translucent and eminently visible apparition of a young girl in white period garb ...

THE *GHOST HUNT* FILES

It was a suitably gloomy and overcast Dunedin afternoon when the *Ghost Hunt* team arrived at the Fortune. Aware of the reputation theatres have for being haunted, Carolyn was rather nervous. But Michael, an actor who has worked the stage himself, felt completely at home. Brad, as the technical specialist, was surprised by the vastness of the former church's interior. Backstage is a multi-level labyrinth of narrow corridors, stairwells and stepladders leading to green rooms, make-up rooms, props rooms and storage spaces of all shapes and sizes. It is a veritable warren of sharp turns and dark corners. There are also no windows backstage, so when the lights are out it's black — pitch black.

Following directions from Andrew Smith, Brad investigated a musty bunker some seven flights below the Carnegie Centre which sits directly across the street from the theatre. It is another haunted spot, allegedly by the spirit of a homeless man who died there — the body was found in such a state of fetid decomposition that he came to be known as the 'liquid man'. Local legend has it that this bunker was built during the Second World War, a fact that could not be corroborated through public record. A small hole in the bunker wall revealed a trickle of running water, purportedly spirit water from a haunted subterranean spring. Brad decided that, in view of the associated stories, it was worth setting up surveillance equipment in this bunker as well as at the Fortune.

The trifield meter which Brad had set up deep below in the bunkers soon began registering exceedingly high amounts of electromagnetic flux. Brad could find no logical explanation for this, and sent Michael to investigate. Although Michael found nothing out of the ordinary, an anomaly was discovered during the *Ghost Hunt* analysis: a fleeting glimpse of what paranormal experts refer to as ectoplasm moving past the camera on one of the landings.

Backstage in the theatre, Carolyn suffered an emotional meltdown:

> *It totally felt like there was some sort of presence there. I didn't see anything. It's just a feeling you get. I heard lots of creaking. And I'm sure I kept hearing a groaning sound. I felt trapped in the dark. It was totally claustrophobic. I just freaked. I couldn't move.*

Eventually Carolyn completely froze, and had to be rescued and led out of the backstage maze by Michael. She emerged from the theatre in tears and visibly shaken. She reported sensing the chilly, lurking presence that witnesses talked about. On closer examination, a photograph taken on the smaller downstairs stage revealed a cluster of orbs to stage left. A stage technician had warned her earlier that this was the section of the stage where many ghostly phenomena occurred.

While Michael was exploring the main stage upstairs, he noticed that all of the audience seating had been folded back except for one, a seat in the centre row about mid-aisle. This prompted Michael and Brad to joke over the two-way radio about the phantom audience member, the angry parishioner. Later on, as Michael attempted to take some photos of the audience seating from the stage, the flash on his camera inexplicably failed (later examination could find no fault with the device). As it was, Michael improvised his shots by utilising an unorthodox technique — holding a torch beneath his camera to provide illumination.

Michael said that at the time he felt no strange presences inside the theatre, and there was no sense of unease while on the stage itself. Accustomed to treading the boards in periods of darkness Michael naturally seemed quite at home. But later, when his photographic efforts were examined, one shot in particular caused Michael some unease. It is a blurry, underexposed shot of the audience seating. In a centre row mid-aisle seat, an indistinct, white-coloured figure is visible, seated and leaning forward angrily. Could this be the ghost of the angry parishioner? Had Michael's flash not suspiciously failed at the crucial moment, what more could have been revealed?

Dunedin's haunted hotspots

If you look at the number of hauntings per regional head of population, Dunedin easily earns the moniker 'New Zealand's most haunted city' (even without taking into account the legendarily haunted Larnach Castle situated just outside town). The highlights of Dunedin include:

- The Dunedin Tourist Information Centre is situated in premises that used to form part of what was the original Dunedin Hospital. This site is alleged to be haunted by a spirit called a 'Grey Lady' (see chapter 2), whose story harks back to a young mother whose baby was taken into care. The mother fell into a depression and soon passed away. While the hospital still operated, nurses reported her pitiful, shadowy ghost wandering the wards, searching for her child. Nurses claim it was not uncommon to feel her tug at them as they walked the wards, especially late in the evening. Eerie sobbing was often heard. Supernatural activity is occasionally reported from the location to this day.
- A first-floor office in the Security Building on Stuart Street was where popular lawyer James Ward was killed in 1962 by a letter bomb. No one was ever arrested for the crime, and the room has supposedly been subject to bizarre phenomena ever since. Many speculate that it is the restless spirit of the legal eagle, still rattled by his sudden and unexpected departure from the realm of the living.
- The Regent Theatre and the Ra Bar next door are both situated on Dunedin's renowned Octagon, a unique octagonal crossroads in the city centre. In 1879 this was the site of one of Dunedin's worst disasters: an arsonist burnt much of the Octagon to the ground and 12 people lost their lives in the blazing inferno. The fire is believed to have been started where the Regent Theatre

now stands. Both theatre and bar are said to be home to paranormal activity — a waitress once ran screaming from the wine cellar of the Ra Bar after witnessing a ghost floating in mid-air on a 'ring of fire'.

- The First Church is allegedly haunted by the ghost of a jilted bride-to-be. The angst of being left standing at the altar drove the poor girl to suicide, and her apparition has been seen standing outside the church, still sadly awaiting her groom.

- Olveston House is one of Dunedin's most magnificent and imposing mansions. Built in the early 1900s by merchant and collector David Theomin, the 35-room house was bequeathed to the city in 1966. Today it operates as a meticulously maintained time capsule, its furnishing and contents little changed since the Great War. Many visitors to Olveston have reported a shadowy figure creeping through its corridors.

- Moray Place, in the centre of Dunedin, leads to an enclosed alleyway said by some locals to be the haunt of a slavering 'demon dog'. The source of this unusual and menacing-sounding haunting is unknown.

Dunedin's inner-city crossroads of the Lower Octagon and Stuart Street, is home to many spirits — a dozen who fell victim to an arson that burned the Octagon to the ground in 1879.

1/1-006136; F. Alexander Turnbull Library, Wellington.

5. riccarton house, christchurch

Not every ghost story stems from a dark and tragic incident. In some cases, the story behind a haunting is one of love, dedication and devotion — the situation of a spirit so attached to the earthly realm that it never wants to leave. This is the case of Christchurch's Riccarton House. This landmark mansion, owned by the founding family of Canterbury, is one of the city's most popular reception houses, fully furnished with antiques and maintained by a private trust. The house is as welcoming as it is beautiful, a place that radiates the warmth, love and close ties to the family that built and lived behind its doors for nearly a century.

Yet behind the exquisite façade of Riccarton House lies the sad tale of a broken heart. It was built in 1855 by Jane Deans in honour of her dead husband, a labour of love fulfilling deathbed plans and promises. This has led many locals to dub Riccarton House the 'Taj Mahal' of Christchurch — a symbol of triumph, tragedy and an enduring, never-ending romance.

The story goes back to the 1840s when two Scottish brothers, John and William Deans, left their homeland for a new life in New Zealand. Having inspected and rejected other parts of the country, the brothers settled on the plains at Putaringamotu, a Maori name meaning 'place of an echo'. The brothers pitched their tent and began construction of the first house to be built on the Canterbury Plains. Once

Haunted historic houses

Why do so many historic houses have their own resident ghosts? More to the point, why are so many old houses that are open to the public allegedly haunted? According to John Webster, the curator of Ewelme Cottage in Parnell, Auckland (see chapter 10), it is because visitors so often come to these places with an expectation to see or experience something — in other words, they like to think the house is haunted and therefore will project feelings and emotions which may result in a manifestation.

Most historic homes open to the public are furnished with antiques and memorabilia that easily transport visitors' thoughts back in time, or are decorated with old photographs and portraits that bring the history of the place alive. It is feasible that these objects and furnishings carry with them some imprint of their past, and subsequently those who are sensitive to psychic energy sense the presence of these former owners.

Paranormal experts speculate that spirits return to places they were extremely happy in, as well places of high drama and tragedy. Old homes undoubtedly have a long history of human activity, and many emotional moments, both happy and sad, take place within their walls. Or, perhaps hauntings are due to the fact that these places are so well cared for that past residents simply don't want to leave — ever!

Like Riccarton House and Ewelme Cottage, many of New Zealand's other historic homes are allegedly haunted. Alberton, a grand colonial mansion in Mt Albert, Auckland, is haunted by the spirit of a former gardener who is often seen peering out of a deep well located on the property. And Highwic, another grand Gothic manor house in Epsom, even has its own ghost dog ...

The Old Stone House in Christchurch, a popular reception room, is said to be haunted by the ghost of an Indian baker who was murdered by a jealous compatriot and burnt in the kitchen oven. Others say that a transparent lady in white haunts its corridors.

New Zealand's oldest stone building, the Stone Store at Kerikeri, recently made headlines when security guards claimed to have seen a grey-haired woman dressed in period garb lurking around the entrance in the dead of night. Nearby historic Kemp House also has a resident spook, the spirit of an old man possibly killed during the Musket Wars of the 1820s.

Objects and furnishings found in historic homes, such as here at Ewelme Cottage (see chapter 10), may carry with them some psychic imprint of their former owners.

the farm was established, they bargained with the local Ngai Tahu owners to lease more land, and in December 1846 a 21-year farm lease was signed for the land running six miles (9.7 km) in every direction from Puturingamotu. The farm was named Riccarton after the Deans' home parish in Scotland, and the nearby river named Avon after the stream on their grandfather's farm.

The Deans became successful farmers, selling their produce in Akaroa and Wellington and their wool in London. It seemed that the hardships associated with pioneering life was paying off but, unfortunately for the two enterprising brothers, tragedy was just around the corner. In 1851 William sailed for Sydney to buy more stock but the ship became wrecked off Cape Terawhiti and he was presumed drowned. William's body was never recovered, leaving John to continue managing the farm alone.

John had other plans, however. Before leaving Scotland he had become enamoured with a young woman he met at a picnic, Jane McIlwraith. It was a typically chaste Victorian relationship and years later Jane would write, 'On the hill we formed our first impressions of each other, he thinking "I would do for New Zealand", I thinking "he looked like the head of a family, so staid and quiet".'

Although not officially engaged, Jane promised to wait for him and they exchanged a love token — a pair of gloves. As it happened, she waited ten years for her pioneering lover to return to collect her. Just six months after his brother's death John boarded a ship bound for Scotland and, after a prolonged separation and three months' travel on six ships, John Deans and Jane McIlwraith were finally reunited on New Year's Day

1852. The patient couple married on 15 September 1852 and a month later they headed to New Zealand.

Pregnant with her first child, it was a long and arduous journey for Jane. Family lore says that she was 'homesick, seasick and morning sick'. Her son, John II, was born on 6 August 1853, six months after arriving in New Zealand. Less than a year later, husband John I contracted tuberculosis and died, leaving Jane literally holding the baby in a simple, one-room cottage, far from family and friends on the other side of the world.

Jane remained in New Zealand, however, and looked after the estate for her son until he was old enough to take it over. Jane had little knowledge of farming — and even less of the strange new country she now lived in — but she soon became a good judge of stock, especially horses and cattle. Through sheer determination, this woman, of tiny stature and frail build, forged an empire that holds an important place in Canterbury society today. According to Graham Hemming, the administration manager of Riccarton House and staff member for 12 years, Jane's story is one of 'Victorian presbyterian Scottish endurance'.

> Life wasn't meant to be enjoyed, it was meant to be endured. She learnt very quickly about life and business and farming and how to endure. What she really had was a sense of duty and purpose. She never married again, and devoted her life to carry on the vision that her husband had.

One of John and Jane's final discussions was about the need for a better house; where it should be built and in what style. Of this Graham says:

They literally made deathbed plans and promises, and that's not dramatic to say that … This place continues their love story. It's a story of dreams and loves and promises. Promises made, and promises kept.

Construction of the house began in 1855 and, at the time, seashells and human hair became inadvertent ingredients in the plaster. The Deans family continued to live in Riccarton House for nearly a hundred years. Jane had 12 grandchildren, and as the family grew, the house was extended. Tragedy continued to dog the family, however, with Jane's son John II dying from meningitis at the age of 48. Jane was to outlive not only her husband but also her son and three grandchildren.

Built in 1855, Riccarton House was home to the Deans family for nearly a century, and tragedy was to dog the family throughout that time. Jane's apparition, described as a figure clad in black, has been witnessed on many occasions on the upper levels.

1/1-004415; G. Alexander Turnbull Library, Wellington.

She died in her bed at Riccarton House at age 87 and was buried alongside her husband in Barbadoes Street Cemetery, 57 years after his death.

Today, every room, corridor and corner of Riccarton House resonates with the memory of this amazing woman, who was to dedicate her life to maintaining Riccarton Bush. According to Dorothy O'Donnell, local psychic and owner of New Zealand's only paranormal website, www.nzghosts.co.nz, Jane's spirit is tangible to everyone who enters the house, speaking to them through the furniture, the photographs, the portraits and the vast collection of Deans family memorabilia:

> You can put your hand on certain pieces of furniture, and you can feel a pulse, the whole living of the place. I think Jane Deans would never want to leave somewhere she put her life and soul into. The first time I went into her bedroom, I could smell violets, and practically sense her standing by the window looking out. There wasn't actually a manifestation, it was just a feeling I got.

Others say that Jane's presence is more than 'just a feeling'. A handful of people (mostly staff members with a long association with the house) have actually witnessed her apparition, described as a black-clad figure, on the upper landing of the house. Graham Hemming has seen the ghost of Jane Deans just once, but has felt her presence many times:

> She was walking down the corridor one afternoon, a lady in a period skirt or dress. It was so real, I followed her into a room to talk to her, but she disappeared. It's a strange feeling – you don't feel that you've seen a spirit, but you know something has happened. And the strange thing is, you don't need to tell anyone about it, and if people don't believe you, you don't care!

Graham tells of another staff member, the catering manager, experiencing an unusual encounter on the first-floor landing:

> *She had locked the house up and was all alone and came up to check that all was well … she turned around to go down the stairs, and behind her she heard a rustling noise. When she turned around, she saw a black skirt and a well-turned ankle swish up the attic stairs … Interestingly, she didn't feel frightened or scared — but she knew it was Jane. We have this theory that you need to do your time here, she'll only appear to you after four or five years. She's a reluctant spirit, but she'll put in an appearance, as if to say 'I'm here'.*

According to the Deans family, the first sighting of Jane Deans occurred in 1915, just four years after her death. One of Jane's great-grandchildren had recently been born, and was being cared for in an upstairs bedroom by the midwife. The midwife observed a little old lady entering the room, looking at the baby, then leaving without saying a word. The midwife, puzzled, described to the family the woman she'd seen and they replied that the description matched Jane. They then showed the midwife a photograph of Jane, and she confirmed that the woman she had seen was the departed family matriarch.

Another inexplicable event occurred in 1998, when Graham Hemming found candlewax on the mantelpiece of the same upstairs bedroom. Since Graham personally locks up every night and knows exactly who is in the building at all times, he knew that nobody had been in the room or had an opportunity to light a candle. The wax appeared where a candelabra used to stand, as if someone had left candles burning till the wax overflowed.

According to Dorothy O'Donnell, Jane Deans may not be the only spirit lingering in Riccarton House. She believes the ghost of a departed cook may still be wandering around the downstairs pantry and cold store, while Graham Hemming has also heard the sound of children's voices upstairs. Considering that three children lived and died in the house, it is feasible that their spirits have returned to this once-happy family home ...

THE *GHOST HUNT* FILES

Hopeless romantics by nature, both Carolyn and Michael were immediately drawn to the tragic love story behind the Riccarton hauntings, entering the house with the belief that Jane Deans might reveal herself to them. From Brad's technical perspective, setting up this investigation was more straightforward than usual since the apparition of Jane tends to appear in specific places. He set up cameras and ghost-hunting apparatus such as an EMF meter in Jane's regular haunts such as the attic, the upstairs landing and the bedroom.

Despite Riccarton House appealing to her sense of aesthetics during daylight hours, Carolyn became extremely jumpy when she entered for her nocturnal investigation. Even the unblinking eyes of the mounted moose and caribou in the front entrance hallway set her on edge. Exploring the Portrait Room on the ground floor, Carolyn felt that the images were poised to jump out of the frames to frighten her.

Meanwhile, Michael had a bizzare experience in one of the upstairs bedrooms, an experience he was completely oblivious to at the time but which Brad captured on one of the night-vision cameras set up on the balcony. Roughly 30 seconds after entering the room from the outside balcony, the door closed behind Michael of its own accord. There were no winds outside at the time, and no other impetus was found that could cause the door to close by itself.

Both Michael and Carolyn felt the strongest energy in the upstairs bedrooms, and in their words the whole house seemed 'alive' — creaking, moaning, weird noises and squeaking. On walking into one room, Michael immediately felt the temperature drop and heard the walls begin to creak loudly. In another bedroom, where Jane slept for 55 years and eventually passed away, both investigators sensed her presence, and felt it appropriate to ask Jane's permission before entering and talked to her during their investigations. Both claimed that they felt intrusive being in Jane's personal space and bid a hasty retreat from the room.

Carolyn's strongest reaction, however, was in the attic where Brad had set up a trifield meter. When the meter began beeping, Brad asked Carolyn to head up there and take some photos. According to Carolyn, her legs felt like jelly and she had to force herself to take every step. On examining the photographs that Carolyn took, Brad noticed a mysterious white mark — an unusual solid ovoid — on the walls above where the trifield meter was placed. Brad suggested that this was ectoplasm caught on film, backing up the evidence of the trifield meter reading and Carolyn's own trepidation on entering the attic.

The most conclusive — and disturbing — evidence from this *Ghost Hunt*, however, came from a photograph that Carolyn took during her daylight exploration of the grounds.

Ectoplasm

Ectoplasm is a cloudy, vaporous mist sometimes appearing in photographs as white smoke or fog. It is said to be the second stage of manifestation after an orb, residual energy manifesting in its basic physical form. The term comes from the Greek words 'ekto' and 'plasma', meaning 'exteriorised substance'. The paranormal use of the term dates back to the early days of spiritualism, when fraudulent mediums used to regurgitate a cheesecloth fabric to display their supposed communication with the dead.

Ectoplasm can also make an appearance in horror movies as either a slimy green trail deposited by ghosts or an ooze emanating from supernatural portals and hellholes. It is often described as having an ozone-like stench. In general, however, it is associated with swirling mists captured on film. It normally appears several metres off the ground and can linger or travel through the air at will. It is more commonly spotted at cemeteries, battlefields and historical sites.

During the *Ghost Hunt* investigations, ectoplasm was captured on a number of occasions. Carolyn photographed a strange, milky substance oozing out of the attic wall at Riccarton House, while a bizarrely floating mist followed Michael down the stairs at the Fortune Theatre (see chapter 4).

A somewhat blurred photo reveals a strange, dark mask-like shape lurking on the balcony behind a bush, a terrifying figure which did not appear in an earlier photo taken at the same location. Could this dark blur be the image of Jane Deans captured on film? Or something more sinister?

The dark, mask-like manifestation, one of several apparitions at Riccarton House, was photographed lurking behind a bush on the balcony.

6. whatipu, west coast auckland

Standing on the deserted black-sand beach at Whatipu, accompanied only by the incessant thunder of the waves pounding the rocky headland and the screech of seabirds, this lonely stretch of coastline feels so remote, so dramatically wild and untouched — little wonder it is considered one of Auckland's secret treasures, a place of refuge for fishermen, hikers and true romantics.

It is also easy to understand why this coastline is considered haunted, both by ancient spirits and ones more recently departed. Everything about the place, the way it looks and feels, seems spiritual and sacred. Not only is it thought of as a place of special significance to Maori, but it is also known for its paranormal activity along the beaches, in the caves, along the tracks ... and in the quaint lodge, the realm of the famous Pink Lady.

Whatipu is located at the northern mouth of the Manukau Heads, a treacherous harbour entrance that has claimed many ships. It is ringed by the pristine, forest-clad Waitakere Ranges, and is characterised by its broad expanse of ironblack sand, endless stretches of wetlands and dramatic headlands and cliffs. Apart from a camping ground, some eclectic baches and the holiday lodge, there are few vestiges of civilisation here. It is difficult to believe this isolated oasis at the end of a dirt track was once a bustling port and timber centre, the hub of a thriving industry.

Paranormal activity often occurs in areas of spiritual and sacred significance — the stretches of black-sand beach and rocky headland caves at Whatipu are home to numerous ancient ghosts.

Despite the overwhelming sensation of isolation, the area has been occupied by humans for over a thousand years. It was a strategic location for Te Kawerau a Maki, the traditional guardians of the Waitakere Ranges. The headland was protected by four pa, and it was the site of several bloody inter-tribal battles. Some of the caves along the coastline were used as burial ground and subsequently became tapu.

Traditional customs tell that Maori spirits journey the length of Aotearoa's west coast, crossing the Manukau Harbour to Whatipu before continuing north to Cape Reinga on their way to join their ancestors. The souls of the dead travel up the coast on a spirit highway, making the entire coastline an extremely sacred place.

It is also said that Kupe, navigator of Polynesia, passed here on his first voyage of discovery and made a sacrifice on Ninepin Rock, the jagged pinnacle in the centre of Whatipu beach. This sacrifice, possibly human, was made to ensure the safety of the travellers on their voyage north.

The Maori name Whatipu is said to come from 'waitipu', meaning the 'stream that rises quickly in flood'. However, there is other speculation that the name is a contraction of 'Te wahi tipua', meaning 'place of demons'. In Maori mythology, this was the place where the taniwha would gather. The continuous process of physical change on the coastline was attributed to these creatures, particularly the taniwha Kawhare, who had lairs both inside the Manukau Harbour and at Piha.

The first Europeans to set foot on the West Coast beaches were a group of missionaries led by Samuel Marsden, who walked the coastline in 1821 while waiting for their schooner, the *Active,* to arrive in New Zealand. By all accounts this first interaction with the local Maori was an amiable encounter. The Manukau Harbour soon became a popular point of entry for ships bringing supplies and passengers from Sydney into New Zealand. Its convenient location on the Tasman meant that the harbour was a preferable option over the longer journey round the northern tip to Auckland. Its entrance, fringed by an ever-shifting bar, was extremely hazardous and many ships ran to ground attempting to enter. Some 233 lives have been lost here in shipwrecks since European habitation of the area.

Ghosts and spirits in Maori folklore

In Maori culture, belief in spirits is intrinsic. Maori believe all living things are descended from the gods, or atua, and embodied in certain mountains, rivers and lakes. All living things possess an inner soul, or wairua, and this is one of the reasons why Maori have such strong spiritual ties to the land. On death, Maori believe that the spirit travels along the west coast of the North Island to the pohutukawa tree that sits at the very tip of Cape Reinga. The spirit then slides down a root of the tree to the sea below before joining their ancestors.

Maori are often reticent to talk about ghosts, or kehua, considering it a tapu subject. Yet the spiritual world is an integral part of their culture and Maori legends are filled with tales of apparitions and paranormal activity. There are numerous tales of Maori warriors appearing at ancient pa sites, or of long-deceased family members appearing as a warning of imminent danger. Kehua are spirits that are never seen during the daytime. They wander around at night, and are very much figures of dread. Kikokiko are more malevolent ghosts that take possession of men and women, causing them to become insane.

Maori also believe in fairy folk and forest spirits. Turehu are ghostly, light-skinned people who live in woodland areas, while the maero is an evil, fierce fairy who inhabits South Island forests. Patupaiarehe are fairy folk who resemble humans and live on hilltops, moving around in the darkness and on misty days. They eat their food raw, covet treasures, or taonga, and are frightened by fire.

There are also various monsters and supernatural creatures that play pivotal roles in traditional Maori culture. The taniwha is a fabulous monster that inhabits rivers, lakes and oceans, sometimes appearing as a whale or shark, sometimes as a dragon and at other times as a floating log. These supernatural beings can be hostile if threatened, but they usually act as guardians of tapu places. So long as they are treated with respect, taniwha do no harm and work to protect the tribe.

Arguably,the most famous New Zealand ghost story is that of the phantom canoe which was observed by many gliding silently across Lake Tarawera, 11 days before the massive volcanic eruption of 1886. This phantom canoe, or waka, was considered an omen, a harbinger of the impending disaster.

The biggest shipping disaster in New Zealand history occurred here in 1863, when the *Orpheus* came to grief off Whatipu. The story of this disaster is a compelling one of miscalculation and bad decisions. The disaster could have been avoided if the captain had sailed into Auckland Harbour — instead, pressed for time, he decided to take on the bar at Manukau. By all accounts it was a calm, sparkling day. The signalman on the shore saw the ship when it was two miles out to sea, giving the signal for the ship to take the bar, indicating that the ship was on the correct course. Commodore Burnett, working off old charts, ignored these signals. Realising that the ship was veering off course, the signalman hoisted another signal to 'keep further offshore'. However, Burnett was unwilling to follow anything but the charts he had, and repeatedly ignored the signals. At 2 p.m. the *Orpheus* struck the sandbank and immediately foundered.

By the time the passing steamer *Wonga Wonga* came to the rescue at 6 p.m., the *Orpheus* was breaking up under the battering of the sea, and three-quarters of the crew had already been lost. A few managed to swim to safety while others clung to floating debris. At 8.30 p.m. the main mast broke and many of the ship's officers — including Commodore Burnett — were swept into the sea. Despite the rescue efforts of the *Wonga Wonga*, of the 259 on board, 189 perished.

> *Throughout the long and silent night*
> *Sad wailing cries were heard*
> *As of men drowning in their might*
> *And screams, like of sea bird.*
>
> *Oh! Weep then for the brave*
> *The gallant firm and true*
> *Who sleep beneath the waves*
> *On the Bar of the Manakau.*
>
> *From The Wreck of the Orpheus by Anon (1863)*

During the following weeks, bodies washed ashore all along the coastline, some up to 45 miles away. In all only 50 bodies were found, some being buried beneath the cliffs at Whatipu's Paratutae Island. The body of the ship's chaplain,

Wood engraving of 'The wreck of H.M.S. Orpheus on Manukau Bar, New Zealand' from Illustrated London News, 1863.
PUBL-0033-1863-437. Alexander Turnbull Library, Wellington.

the Reverend Charles B. Haslewood, washed up on the beach six weeks later — mysteriously, his body was perfectly preserved. Seventeen years later, the full-length skeleton of the assistant sailing master, Mr W. Taylor, was unearthed by children playing in the dunes at Piha. The skeleton was still wearing his jacket and boots.

The signalman, the famed mariner and cartographer Captain Thomas Wing, and his son Edward (on duty at the time and the first to see the ship moving towards the bar), were exonerated during the official enquiry into the disaster. The blame was attributed to incorrect charts and primitive signal equipment.

But according to local legend there may have been a

more sinister reason behind the disaster. The day before the shipwreck occurred, Pakeha settlers had felled a sacred fertility tree on Puketutu Island. Devastated by this loss, local Maori had declared an utu, or retribution, for the act. Some say that the *Orpheus* disaster was payback for the lack of respect.

According to the Mayor of Waitakere City, Bob Harvey, Whatipu is 'a coast of ghosts', a place where many lives have been lost and where many souls linger. He believes that these spirits are recognisable to anyone with a connection to the land. In his book, *Untamed Coast*, Bob writes, 'At Whatipu, to stand on this immensity of beach is to feel the body diminished, the soul enlargened. It feels like a very special place.' Many years ago, Bob had these feelings confirmed, in what he describes as a paranormal experience:

> I came out with a mate one night about 15 years ago, and we just walked down the beach talking. We came into an area where we could see massive surf, but we couldn't hear it. Both of us surf and swim, so we know that big waves make big sounds – yet we were in an absolute zone of silence … It was like standing in front of a giant movie screen where we were watching something happen, but the sound wasn't turned on.

The two men continued walking, and then the sound returned. They went back and marked the spot with a stick for future reference. Later, Bob asked a Maori friend what could possibly be the explanation for this phenomenon. His friend explained that this part of the coastline is a 'highway for the spirits' making their way up the coast to Cape Reinga. His friend believed that Bob had actually passed into this zone as something significant was happening.

Waitakere City Mayor Bob Harvey talks of Whatipu as being a 'coast of ghosts', and describes a paranormal encounter of his own.

Famous New Zealanders and ghost sightings

Mayor Bob Harvey is not the only well-known New Zealander with a belief in the paranormal. Some of New Zealand's most prominent citizens have had an encounter with ghosts at some point in their lives.

The conqueror of Mt Everest, Sir Edmund Hillary, has spoken of an encounter with the ghost of Sir Ernest Shackleton, who died in 1916 during an expedition to Antarctica. Sir Edmund claims that he experienced the apparition when he first visited the hut at Ross Island during the 1950s.

Acclaimed film director, Peter Jackson, built his career around the horror genre, breaking through into Hollywood with the 1996 release of *The Frighteners*. What few people realise, however, was that this movie was inspired by a real-life experience: both Jackson and wife Fran witnessed the apparition of a screaming woman's face on two separate occasions.

New Zealand-born soprano, Dame Kiri Te Kanawa, was performing at Edinburgh's Usher Hall in May 2005 when she heard footsteps behind her on stage. She was so disturbed by the occurrence that Dame Kiri interrupted the performance to ask the audience if they had heard them too. Some answered in the affirmative and the shaken opera singer continued, fully believing she was in the presence of a paranormal entity.

From the 1860s until 1916, Whatipu was a productive and busy timberyard with its own mill and wharf. Freshly hewn kauri logs were stacked along the beach waiting to be transported to Onehunga, where they would then be sent to build the cities of Wellington, Christchurch and Dunedin. In its timber-milling heyday, a tram snaked its way along the shoreline from Karekare, operational only at low tide. The wharf was located beside the Paratutae headland. All that remains there now is a few sleepers, some iron rings and a couple of wooden stakes.

In 1921, the last cut timber was shipped out from Paratutae wharf, and ten years later, the last raft of logs was taken to the Onehunga mills. Whatipu was allowed to return to its natural state, the forest again reclaiming its dominance

The beach tramway that connected Karekare with Whatipu during its years as a busy timberyard was usable only at low tide.
APG-0351-1/2 G. Alexander Turnbull Library, Wellington.

of the landscape. The only remaining building from the timber-milling days is the original house, known as Whatipu Lodge.

It was built in 1860 by the Gibbons family, who operated the mill in the valley behind the house. It was originally occupied by Nicholas Gibbons, his wife Matilda and their children. In 1910, Nicholas' son Fred added bunkhouse cabins to accommodate visitors, workers and holidaymakers who were beginning to discover the wild delights of Whatipu. It was during this busy period that the dining room, kitchen and extra accommodation were built.

Despite the good times, life at Whatipu was still quite primitive. Communication with the outside world was sporadic, and transport heavily dependent on the state of the

Whatipu Lodge was built first in 1860 by the Gibbons family,

weather. Stories were told of how pregnant women would not risk the treacherous bridle track and instead travelled down to the wharf for the boat journey to Onehunga.

Fred Gibbons and his family were no strangers to tragedy. In the early twentieth century, all eight of his children contracted diphtheria. Fred took the worst affected children in a flat-bottomed dinghy and rowed to Cornwallis, where they proceeded by cart and boat to Auckland. Battling against the tide, the journey took 14 hours. One of the children died en route, and another in hospital the following day. Such were the tragedies faced by families living in isolated areas in those days.

In 1922, after milling finished, the tram track was closed and the tracks pulled up and sold. Whatipu again became a lonely outpost, with only the Gibbons family remaining. Fred was 57 when the milling ceased, but he and his wife Laura tried to generate business by establishing their lodge as a holiday home. With the road completed in 1920, visitors no longer had to rely on boat transport and Whatipu became known as an exciting and interesting place to stay. During these halcyon days, dances and social occasions were often held in a large cave located about half a kilometre along the coast. There was even a kauri dancefloor laid in the cave, which has long since disintegrated owing to the ravages of time, tide and shifting sands.

The Gibbons family was linked to the lodge for over four generations. Fred and Laura eventually moved away in 1929, selling to an Auckland watchmaker. This was a short-lived venture for the city businessman, and the lodge passed through several hands before ending up in the care of Phil Sharp in 1951, who would run the place for the next 33 years. In 1984 Whatipu Lodge was taken over by Neil and Mary Roberts. They stayed on until 2002, when the Auckland Regional Council acquired the lease.

Even today, the influence of the Gibbons family is evident at the lodge. The original homestead is decorated with their old furnishings, and photographs of the lodge's early days and portraits of family members stare down from the walls. The whole place carries comforting flashbacks to simpler times.

According to Mary Roberts, there is one Gibbons family member who appreciates her home being left in its original state. Mary believes that the lodge is haunted by a spirit known as the Pink Lady, a translucent female apparition with a distinct pink aura who makes the occasional appearance, usually during daylight hours, and only to women or children. Mary has personally witnessed the Pink Lady on two occasions, both during the day, and states emphatically:

> I think the Pink Lady is a member of the Gibbons family … Certainly the person I've experienced here has been older, definitely female, and I think definitely at home here. Certainly when she comes here it's not in a threatening manner — she feels like she's here for a reason, just to look around … My first experience was after we'd been here about six months, and that was a time we spent cleaning. There hadn't been a woman here in a long time. I came into the loungeroom one afternoon about 3 o'clock in the afternoon, and there was definitely a woman in this room. It really felt like she was just watching what I was doing.

Mary can only speculate on the identity of the Pink Lady. It could be the original owner, Matilda Gibbons, or perhaps another family member who had a particular attachment to Whatipu. 'You just knew it was a woman, and you knew she was old. She had long hair tied up, and she has a pink aura. That's why she didn't feel threatening,' Mary says. After the first sighting, she tried to convince herself she had simply imagined the apparition. However, other people — particularly children — began to report seeing a strange old lady in the lodge, vindicating what Mary experienced:

> The most amazing experience occurred one Friday night, when we had a group staying for the weekend. There was lots of children in the group, playing hide and seek. There was a little boy in the loungeroom, covering his eyes and counting to ten. But he didn't come out when he was supposed to, and the other children were calling out for him. I walked into the room, and the little boy was standing here just looking around him, and I knew what had happened … He said, 'There's been a lady in this room. She went out, but she didn't go out through the door. She just disappeared …' I think that was what convinced me that what was happening to me was also happening to other people.

Examination of the Whatipu Lodge guest-book reveals that sightings of the Pink Lady have continued for years, even up to current times. In one contemporary report, a young girl had been playing with her tea set, pouring tea for two. Her mother asked who the other setting was for, and the girl replied that it was for the old lady who wandered around the lodge ...

There have also been some interesting photographs taken in and around the lodge to back up claims of paranormal activity. A rather disturbing sequence shows a mirror which appears to be melting — taken when the photographer felt like she was being pulled 'into a vortex, as though time had stopped'.

Another series of photographs, taken by trampers in the surrounding forest in the dead of night, shows what appears to be demonic images emerging from the blackness. Such proof is entirely circumstantial, but certainly provided a provocative basis for further exploration.

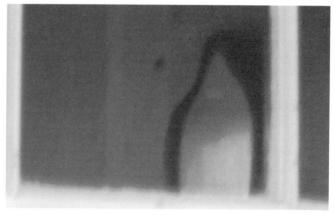

One of many paranormal events occuring around Whatipu Lodge was captured in this disturbing sequence of images depicting a melting mirror.

THE *GHOST HUNT* FILES

The beach, wetlands, dunes and caves of Whatipu have all been zoned part of a scientific reserve by the Department of Conservation (DoC). These areas are off-limits for filmmakers, so Brad was unable to set up cameras in certain allegedly haunted locations. Fortunately, he was able to access the gorge that runs behind Whatipu Lodge, reportedly a paranormal hotspot. This was where the trampers took the photos revealing grotesque demonic images, and it was also where many of the bodies from the wreck of the *Orpheus* washed ashore.

During the nineteenth century, the shoreline came up as far as the lodge and the cliff face. Photographs taken during the milling days show the tram-track hugging the cliff, but with waves lapping at the base of the tracks. Since then, storm activity, shifting sands and the ever-changing currents have resulted in the shoreline receding for almost a kilometre. The lodge now nestles inland behind a vegetated dune system and a huge expanse of black-sand beach.

From Brad's perspective, this shoot was one of the most technically challenging because of the vast amount of ground to cover. To ensure there was ample surveillance coverage, nearly 20 cameras were set up both in the gorge and inside the lodge.

For Michael, the journey into the forest at night was accompanied by a 'strong sense of the land here, but also at the same time, it is full of tragedy, bloodshed'. At first he felt at ease in the forest at night, listening to the distant sounds of the waves and the noises of night birds and creatures scampering around him. As the silence enveloped him, however, he began to get a sense that he was not alone in the gorge that night.

'It's really quite peaceful, but at the same time, you feel like something is watching you,' he said. Photographs taken in infra-red mode on his camera that night reveal strange white figures in a sea of blackness – small, amusing-looking figures resembling spirits or creatures of some description. Michael described one as a 'little gremlin', with a grinning face and jolly countenance. Certainly not a threatening image, but curious nonetheless.

Brad speculated that these figures could be evidence of spiritual activity in the forest, claiming that 'all the photographs seem very ethereal, very spiritual, which matches up to what everyone has been saying about the spirit highway'. Likewise, Carolyn was feeling edgy in the lodge as she recounted tales of the Pink Lady. As she was descending the narrow staircase in the main building, she heard a door close by itself downstairs. Later, Carolyn felt very uncomfortable in the room where the melting mirror photographs were taken. However, her worst fears were realised when Brad sent her back into the dining hall to check a temperature reading. As she came through the kitchen, Carolyn thought she saw movement over by the billiard table. Further investigation revealed nothing, but as she passed by the table, a pool cue propped against the table crashed to the floor. That was enough for Carolyn, and without stopping to investigate further she bolted for the safety of the Ghostmobile.

The video replay reveals that the cue fell *after* Carolyn had passed it. One would assume that if the pack she was wearing on her back touched the cue it would have been dragged *towards* her. Instead, it fell backwards ... the work of a playful poltergeist?

The weirdest evidence gathered in this *Ghost Hunt* is also

Infra-red footage

Infra-red is an invisible portion of the light spectrum extending from 0.75 to 1000 microns, a wavelength longer than visible light but shorter than microwave or higher-frequency radiation. The name means 'below red' (from the Latin 'infra', meaning 'below', and red being the colour of visible light of the longest wavelength). All objects warmer than absolute zero naturally emit infrared energy.

Infra-red is used in night-vision equipment, when there is insufficient light to see an object with the unaided eye. Infra-red cameras also detect radiation caused by electromagnetic fields, creating an image 100 times more powerful than the human eye. In other words, it can pick out an object in the pitch black that a normal camera setting is incapable of seeing. As paranormal experts believe that a spirit is composed of energy that is not visible to the human eye, infrared photography becomes a useful tool in a ghost-hunting expedition.

possibly the most compelling, specifically a photograph that Carolyn took during daylight hours in her bedroom at the lodge. Admiring the quaint, old-fashioned décor, Carolyn had taken a 'happy snap', facing towards the window and looking outwards. The result was a slightly blurry image, strongly backlit by a flare of light coming through the window. What is more bizarre is the elongated figure that appears to be floating mid-air, sitting just inside the window frame. A head, torso and legs are discernible, and the figure is distinctly pink in appearance. Carolyn speculated that this could be the apparition of the Pink Lady, perhaps the ghost of Matilda Gibbons, captured on film:

> I can't believe that that came up in the photo – but the lodge did always feel to me like someone was watching over it and making sure it was properly run, so I can understand why Matilda would want to check up on me as well.

This apparition of head, torso and legs could be Whatipu's legendary Pink Lady, reputedly a member of the Gibbons family who lived at the lodge for four generations.

7. st bathans, central otago

Population: 12 (living souls: 6, lingering spirits: 6).

What self-respecting ghost town would find itself without a restless spirit or two of which to boast? Certainly not St Bathans. At last count it was home to half a dozen alleged ghosts, a figure that matches the living population in the town. And within its one and only pub, the Vulcan Hotel, lurks one of New Zealand's most infamous and persistently reported apparitions. Known simply as the Rose, the Vulcan's supernatural resident is said to be an angry she-spirit with a violent streak, whose sad story is inextricably entwined with the area's gold rush history.

It was in the mid-1800s that gold rushes became quite frequent throughout the South Island. The rush to the town that would come to be known as St Bathans began in 1862, when Irish prospector Peyman unearthed several high-quality nuggets in the area. Mining concentrated on Kildare Hill, and as the miners arrived the town grew alongside it. Within a short space of time, St Bathans was a robust and bustling mining centre with a population of two thousand hardy souls — a motley collection of drifters, grifters and other assorted hopefuls bent on finding their fortune. The principal mining technique employed was hydraulic sluicing, which involved high-pressure jets of water carving away at cliff walls to tap veins of gold.

SLUICING FOR GOLD.

In the 1860s, hydraulic sluicing was the method employed to tap into rich veins of gold found throughout St Bathans.

MNZ-0430-1/4 F. Alexander Turnbull Library, Wellington.

In its heyday, St Bathans would have been more accurately described as spirited rather than spirit-infested. A report filed by the correspondent to the *Cromwell Argus* in 1870 vividly sets the scene:

> In the very centre of the township there stands conspicuously a huge pig style [sic], generally full of fat pigs, and surrounded by the heads and horns of animals. The effluvium rising of the locality on a warm day is enough to create a malarious fever; it is positively sickening. Passing hurriedly by, the stranger carefully guides his horse through the labyrinth of broken bones, bottles, salmon tins and miscellaneous rubbish until he emerges into an esplanade a degree more healthy than the street behind him.

And where there's gold, there's sin — at one point the tent city of St Bathans boasted over a dozen pubs and three dance halls, replete with an endless supply of dancing girls. Houses of ill-repute were numerous, most no more than gaudily daubed corrugated iron facades with canvas walls. Not that it mattered to the miners — even a small nugget of gold could pay for a big night in the boomtown of St Bathans. And in addition to the decadence, deceit and depravity expected of any frontier town, crime flourished. Rape, theft and murder — St Bathans saw it all.

At some point in the early 1880s, the ill-fated Rose drifted into this seedy milieu. Her real name is lost in the dust of time, but the one most commonly known is Jeannie. She was one of an endless stream of young women lured to the minefields with gold dust in their eyes, seeking, presumably, a fresh start in life with a newly rich husband. Instead, Jeannie found work as a dance-hall hooker, and a fast track to her death.

The St Bathans dance halls provided an invaluable social function. Gold miners worked hard under dangerous conditions; one misstep and they could slide in front of the dreaded sluice to be cut in half. Exhausted men working close to death needed to let off steam, to drink to excess, carouse loudly and be entertained by saucy stage acts. After entrancing miners with their onstage charms, dance-hall girls generally had little trouble enticing them back to their tents or tiny hotel rooms for further paid entertainment.

The Rose worked the dance halls and eventually rented a room at the Vulcan. She left no photographic legacy, but legend describes her as a tall 23-year-old with a pretty face and a body abundant with physical attributes. One historical source has it that the Rose was a gifted chanteuse, her dulcet tones renowned throughout the Otago goldfields. It

St Bathans flourished for over 70 years and the Vulcan Hotel, pictured here, is the only hotel to survive those goldrush days.
1/2-027127; F. Alexander Turnbull Library, Wellington.

was said that after an onstage performance the dance hall's rear would be crammed with 'stage door johnnies' eager to experience her charms in a more personal setting.

It was among these men that the Rose sourced her clientele, until one fateful evening she invited the wrong 'john' back to her room. She was found strangled the next morning on the bed in which she earned her living. She had been raped, and all her money, gold and jewellery stolen. Her murderer was never caught.

Gold mining continued with gusto in St Bathans until 1935. Not that the gold veins dried up, but because the sluicing of the 120-metre-tall Kildare Hill had reduced it to a pit 70 metres deep, and the town's main street was in danger of sinking into the chasm. Mining ceased and the pit was flooded. Today it is known as Blue Lake, renowned for its preternaturally blue water.

The township duly shrank to a sad speck of its former self. The only hotel that survived from those halcyon days is the Vulcan, and the Rose has become its most renowned occupant. Reputedly, her spirit manifests itself in the front corner room where the murder occurred, these days known simply as Room Number One.

Not surprisingly, the Rose appears to be a troubled and vengeful ghost out to vent her spiritual spleen particularly on the male of the species, and her spirit can be physically felt as well as seen. Her favourite trick is to climb atop a male asleep in Room Number One and throttle him till he awakens, out of breath, with an icy weight bearing down upon his chest. In some cases male guests find themselves sporting bruises and scratches. Nocturnal occurrences similar to this have been reported by such varied sources as an eminent archaeologist and the lead singer of a well-known rock band. A respected Australian businessman staying in this room also awoke to discover a deep gash made in his flesh, just above the groin.

There is no doubt that a high malevolence factor is involved in this haunting, and there are two schools of thought on the matter: one is that the Rose's behaviour resembles poltergeist activity; another that it is indicative of a more sinister type of spirit, the succubus.

The Rose has made her presence known to women as well, but the manifestations seem to be far less aggressive. Housekeeper Karen Carney was subject to a bizarre experience as she was making the bed in Room Number One of the Vulcan. Of its own accord, a pillowcase stood up on its end and waved at her, apparently for several seconds. The incident wasn't overtly malicious, but it was enough to send Karen scurrying from the room in horror.

Another time she was chatting in the formal dining room with Jude Kavanagh, co-owner of the Vulcan, when they witnessed a female apparition glide across the room and disappear into a corner. Both ladies saw the spirit clearly and were able to corroborate each other's descriptions — quite

Succubus

According to medieval legend, a succubus is a demon or ghost in female form that appears to men through their dreams. It seduces the man into having sexual activity, drawing energy from him to sustain itself — succubi are sometimes described as being capable of sucking the very soul out of a man. According to the infamous tome *Malleus Maleficarum* (or 'Witch's Hammer'), a succubus would collect sperm from men as they slept and then pass the fluid on to an incubus (the male equivalent of the succubus), who would then use it to impregnate unsuspecting women as they slept, in the process creating evil 'demonseed' offspring. In the sixteenth century, a carving of a succubus outside an inn indicated an establishment operating as a brothel.

tall, in her early twenties and clad in a flowing white, period-style dress.

Another staff member saw a figure of similar description sitting alone in a lounge against the wall of the formal dining room. She assumed she was a member of a tour group, only to discover the entire tour group had checked out of the hotel hours earlier. On returning to the dining room the staff member was terrified to find that the young woman had vanished into thin air.

Yet another staff member, after working late, decided to stay overnight rather than travel home. Despite having heard stories of the Rose from others, she and her partner opted for Room Number One. That night they found themselves terrorized by mysterious goings-on in the room next door:

> First we heard footsteps. Then they stopped. Then we could hear what sounded like something being tossed around. The next morning we investigated, and discovered books and magazines strewn all over the floor of the room next door. The scary thing is, we were the only occupants in the hotel that night. The room next door was locked, and neither of us heard the door opening or closing. And the keys to all the other rooms were with us in Room Number One.

Corridors groan, kettles boil without being plugged in and the doors have an annoying habit of locking themselves ... the Vulcan Hotel seems to be a hotbed of spiritual activity. But can all the shenanigans be attributed to the Rose? The Vulcan has become a kind of mini-Mecca for psychics and clairvoyants. One visiting psychic sensed the presence of two additional spirits, usually found huddled over their pints at the bar. According to the psychic, their names are Thomas and Elva. Normally this ghostly couple do not manifest themselves in the form of apparitions, but on some occasions an old timer calling himself Thomas has helped a drunken out-of-towner find his way to the toilet. When they enquire about their kindly benefactor the next morning, they learn that there is no elderly local called Thomas ...

A few years ago, visiting psychics Barbara and Barry Newman set out to investigate supernatural activity in the Vulcan. One of the techniques they employed was to set up a camera to automatically snap a photograph at regular intervals in front of the hotel. In one photograph, an odd mist appears in the corner of one of the windows. The Newmans believe that, when studied closely, the ghostly face of a gold miner is revealed in the mist.

Another nearby haunted site is the historic public hall beside the hotel. Visitors often hear the sound of spectral music and laughter emanating from behind its locked doors. A former local claims to have witnessed here an apparition of a man in army uniform dancing with a little girl to a ghostly piano tune.

An impressive collection of spooks for such a small town, but the queen of the St Bathans spirits is undoubtedly the Rose, and there is a local legend that makes her story even more chilling. Many years ago, workers cleaning up the local cemetery situated on a small hill behind the hotel came across an unmarked and overgrown grave. It was in the much older section of graves, indicating that it dated back to the

1800s. Permission was given to open the casket, and when the lid was pried open it revealed the corpse of a tall young woman. How could they tell she was young? Despite having been in the ground for over a hundred years, the corpse had barely deteriorated ...

THE *GHOST HUNT* FILES

A *Ghost Hunt* researcher arrived in St Bathans a day ahead of the production team. She dutifully booked herself into Room Number One to do some first-hand research on its haunted reputation. She did not enjoy a peaceful night's sleep:

> I woke up around 3 a.m. when I heard all this creaking, like footsteps in my room. It honestly sounded like someone walking around. It was as though they were pottering and trying not to disturb me. You know how girls fiddle around for ages when they're getting ready to go out? And it was definitely a female presence. I just hid under the covers. I peaked but couldn't see anything. I was lying there terrified, wanting for it to go away. But it kind of felt like it was being quite respectful, and trying not to wake me ... And here's the thing: it didn't go on for only a few seconds, it went on for over half an hour. My overall impression was that it was the Rose doing her hair and make-up before heading to work. Then it sounded like the tap on the sink in the corner of my room had been turned on. I could hear gurgling water. And then it stopped. The first thing I did the next morning was to check the sink. It was bone dry. There was even a fine layer of dust on it.

On his arrival in St Bathans, Michael was somewhat disturbed to hear the researcher's story since he had been nominated to spend the next night in the room. On hearing the news his response was, 'You mean, I'm the bait?' Brad gathered Michael and Carolyn together in the Vulcan's bar to examine evidence the Kavanaghs had collected over the years. This included a framed painting, faithfully replicating a photograph taken one night by a tourist at the Vulcan Hotel. Clearly evident in the foreground is a shrouded black figure, lurking outside the window of Room Number One. The other is an antique chocolate box, the cover of which is adorned with an old photograph of the Vulcan Hotel in the snow. A wagon wheel is framed in the foreground, and the melting snow on the wagon wheel appears to take the shape of a pretty female face. The face is looking directly at the camera, and is positioned directly below the Rose's window in the background.

While at the bar Brad was privy to a colourful piece of local folklore from an unnamed regular:

> Contrary to popular belief, there were actually a few deaths when they were sluicing for gold across the road, in the early days. But they weren't officially reported. If a fella fell in front of the sluice, he'd be cut to ribbons, and his body would get sucked into the sludge pit beneath it. It was like quicksand, and it'd be too expensive to shut down operations and dredge the body up. Plus there was a good chance they wouldn't be able to find them anyway. So they just left them there, and reported them missing. Miners were pretty itinerant back then anyway, always drifting off to different digs without giving notice. So as far as the authorities knew, they'd just wandered off. But as far as I've heard, they're still at the bottom of Blue Lake.

Brad was unsure whether or not to take this tale with a grain of salt, but it did seem to fit in with stories of campers who, staying overnight by the lake, witnessed the apparition of a miner emerging from its waters. With this in mind, Brad set up surveillance equipment on the lakeshore and inside the hotel as well as in the dance hall next door.

The night spent in St Bathans during the investigation was a strange and perplexing one. While setting up equipment outside in the Ghostmobile, Brad heard weird sounds emerging from the trees situated between the hotel and the lake. On investigating, Brad sensed a presence, as though he was being watched, and heard footsteps that seemed to be very close, circling him — yet no nearby movement was discernible. Carolyn was shocked by a loud, unexplained thump while investigating the public hall — there appeared to be no explanation for it. She emerged shaken only to find herself encircled by the same invisible footsteps as she headed down the town's main street back to the van.

While investigating the hotel, Michael also heard a mysterious noise, what sounded like a teacup clinking in the formal dining room. His night's sleep in Room Number One was marred by unexplained scratching sounds on the front window. Production crew members in the corridor outside the room witnessed, as previously reported by Karen Carney, a kettle turning itself on. They examined it and confirmed that it was not plugged in to an electric socket. They also heard what they described as 'anguished female moaning' from both ends of the same corridor.

Further into the evening's investigation, Brad detected an unusually high reading for electromagnetic flux emanating from the shoreline of the lake. Michael investigated, and braved a midnight dip in the dark, chilly waters. During

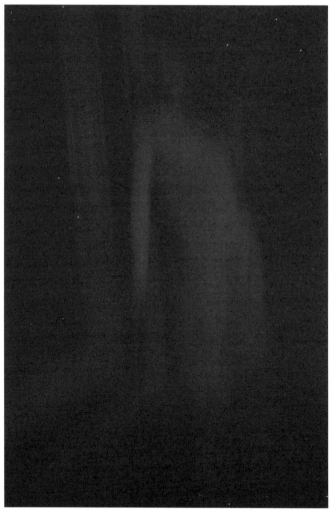

This image of a female apparition resembles Rose, a former dance-hall hooker brutally murdered at the Vulcan Hotel in the late nineteenth century.

an analysis of some underwater photographs, a barely discernible shape became apparent. Brad noted that part of the shape seemed to resemble a miner's helmet, but owing to the low-light conditions under which the photograph was taken, this could not be confirmed.

A more startling image was discovered on analysing Michael's photographs taken inside the hotel. After investigating the clinking sound in the dining room, he had snapped a couple of shots — one with a flash and one without. The photograph taken without the flash was dark and hazy, but on being digitally brightened it shows what appears to be the misty image of a woman, her face grey and undefined, standing in the corner of the room in what can only be described as a 'come hither' pose. Even Brad was flummoxed, but as he pointed out, the lines of the wall in the background are clearly defined, therefore the streaks in the image could not be attributed to camera movement. Michael's summation was succinct: 'It is what it is. It's an apparition of a woman.' The Rose, finally caught on camera? Or simply a blurry shadow?

Haunted pubs of New Zealand

It seems that the appeal of alcohol is such that it extends into the afterlife! It is a worldwide phenomenon that many hotels and pubs are paranormal hotspots, perhaps because of the warmth of the establishment, the welcoming nature of the building and the hospitality shown, or perhaps because they are so often the scene of highly charged emotions, with fights and brawls breaking out from an over-indulgence in alcoholic spirits. Whatever the reason for this phenomenon, New Zealand's pubs and taverns are no exception. As well as the famed Vulcan Hotel in Central Otago, there are countless historic pubs said to house at least one ghost, often the victim of foul play during wilder times.

New Zealand's oldest licensed hotel, the Hurunui Hotel, in the backcountry of Canterbury, is a welcoming watering hole with a dark secret. It is said to be haunted by Charlotte, the spirit of a maid who disappeared under mysterious circumstances at the end of the nineteenth century. She is said to still inhabit Room 13, and occasionally pays a visit to the bar for light entertainment.

Another historic pub with its own resident spook is the Blackball Hilton in the West Coast town of Blackball. This place is haunted by the spirit of a woman who has a tendency to lock doors and send glasses crashing from shelves in the bar. Many guests have sensed a presence in the upstairs guestrooms, with a common complaint being that someone was standing over them watching them sleep.

The Granity Tavern, also on the West Coast of the South Island, has had a colourful and tragic past. In 1929 a fire broke out in the hotel killing six guests, some of whom appear to have chosen to linger in its icy corridors and rooms. The epicentre of the paranormal activity is outside Room 16, where history says an 18-year-old coalminer became trapped and died.

The Brian Boru Hotel in Thames is the oldest Irish pub in New Zealand. Built in 1868, it burnt down in 1900 when the cook fell asleep in the kitchen while tending the open fire. Two visitors staying upstairs were also killed in this tragedy, and it is said that the hotel is haunted by these two spectres, as well as the ghost of the former owner's wife, who likes to move furniture around in upstairs guest rooms.

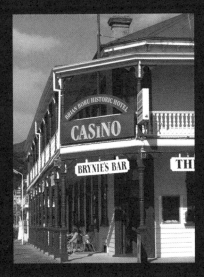

Two guests killed in a tragic fire at Thames' Brian Boru Hotel in 1900 are said to still haunt the building.

8. waikumete cemetery, glen eden, auckland

There seem to be two schools of thought regarding cemeteries and ghosts. One is that cemeteries, as places where souls are put to rest, are not where restless spirits are likely to be found. The other way of thinking is more direct: where you find the dead, you will find ghosts. Sprawling Waikumete Cemetery, situated on the outskirts of Auckland, is a burial ground with more than enough ghostly stories attached to make one believe the latter.

Waikumete is by far the largest cemetery in New Zealand. When describing its sheer size, the term 'necropolis' springs to mind. Its expansive, rolling hills and steep gullies cover more than 120 hectares, the average size of a suburb, and is dotted with graves as far as the eye can see.

Originally known as Waikomiti, it was established in 1886 to accommodate spill-over from Grafton Cemetery, which at the time was becoming congested. The vacant site was chosen owing to its proximity to the Helensville–Auckland railway line, and its lack of proximity to the city centre. Perched on the very edge of the cemetery, Glen Eden railway station was originally built six years previously in 1880, and the development of the area was inextricably bound with that of the cemetery and the railroad. An 1886 item in the *Weekly News* optimistically prophesied: 'The rites, ceremonies and requirements of the cemetery will be sure to attract residents to the township, and so around the city of the dead will arise a new city for the living.'

But, as it turned out, population growth in the surrounding suburb stymied. After all, who wants to live in a town named after a cemetery? The rather pretty name Glen Eden was chosen after the First World War, and since then has developed into a healthy, bustling suburb — a suburb built on the business of death.

Today, the giant graveyard is surrounded by suburbia on all sides. A stroll through Waikumete Cemetery would take up most of a day, and even at that rate one could not to take in all the detail. It is divided into numerous sections according to religious denomination, and monuments vary from enormous mausoleums to crude, homemade headstones. But the section of most interest, due in no small part to the fact that it is purported to be the most haunted, is what is known simply as the 'old section'.

When the railway station was first built near to this older section, a siding platform was constructed to facilitate the lifting of coffins. The disused platform sits there today, blended into the industrial surrounds, the rails and siding facilities long removed. The new Glen Eden railway station, boasting the original historic station house, is 200 metres further up the track.

In days gone by, coffins were carried in boxcars with doors marked with white crosses, and mourners would travel by ordinary carriage on the same train. It took an entire day for mourners to journey with their loved one to the cemetery, hold the funeral service, and return again by train to the city. Caskets were taken either to the Mortuary Chapel for the service or straight to the grave by horse-driven hearse. The coffins of paupers were loaded onto wheelbarrows and trundled into the cemetery.

This system was turned into chaos during the Spanish influenza epidemic of 1918, to which over 5000 New Zealanders lost their lives. Approximately 1600 of these are buried at Waikamete, and the rapidity with which the epidemic spread stretched the resources of the day far too thin. A shortage of cemetery staff and a lack of building materials for coffins meant that corpses piled up in and around the station for days at a time. It was reported to be a sad, horrific sight and the stench of death was overwhelming. Local resident Bert Southgate remembers those awful days:

> I was working on the pig cart at the time, and people were dropping dead around town. You'd see a fellow walking along, and all of a sudden he would stagger and go down — wallop! There was a train that came out to Glen Eden with two carriages full of the dead. There were no crematoriums in those days, and they couldn't dig the graves fast enough. They used to take the bodies and put them under trees behind the station until they had time to turn around and bury them.

The result was that many of the victims were buried in a mass grave, some in hastily banged together coffins, and others with no casket at all. A sad, solitary, stone monument now marks the site atop an eerie expanse of bare lawn at the cemetery.

Casting a shadow over this section of the cemetery are the looming ghost gums of Murderers' Grove. This is where 19 executed killers — deliberately refused markers — either were buried or had their ashes scattered. In Waikumete's first year of operation, John Caffey and Albert Penn (hanged for killing a fellow workman on a Shortland Street building site) were allegedly buried upright so that their spirits would never find rest. Legend has it that grass will not grow over their graves, and dogs reputedly avoid those particular spots.

Curiously enough the ashes of Walter James Bolton (in February 1957 to be the last man hanged in New Zealand) were not scattered here. In a strange twist, they were returned to his family and interred in the same plot as his wife — the woman he was convicted of killing. Victims of murder are buried here as well; the grave of one victim, Horatio Heywood Frecherville Ramsden, displays the rancorous epitaph, 'Vengeance is mine'.

It is worth noting another macabre tale, an incident of grave-robbing. In 1939 an Australian visitor, Mr G.R. Mackay, was apparently burnt to death in a fire in a Piha bach. His friend, Mr J. Talbot, allegedly attempted his rescue but was unsuccessful owing to the intense heat. A toothless skull was the only object retrieved from the ashes. But the plot thickened ...

Police were puzzled as to why Mr Mackay's dentures, which should have withstood the inferno, were not found. And also as to why the skull had pieces of cotton wool wedged in the palate, as though it were taken from a body professionally laid out by a mortician. The £40,000 life insurance policy recently taken out by Mackay also looked suspicious.

An elderly woman recognised the faces of Mackay and Talbot from a newspaper report as the gentlemen who had hired a garage from her, and duly reported to authorities. Police discovered a shovel wrapped in a sack concealed in the garage. An analysis of a clay sample taken from the shovel revealed that it came from Waikumete Cemetery. They enlisted the help of the cemetery's sexton, who led them to the grave of a certain Mr Shine, only recently laid to rest, and who had been known to wear dentures but had been buried without them. Mr Shine's grave was duly dug up and discovered to be empty!

The plot finally unravelled. Talbot and Smith had attended Mr Shine's funeral and learned that he wore false teeth. That night they returned to the cemetery, exhumed his body, stashed it in the bach and set it alight in order to claim it was the body of Mackay. The two grave robbers were eventually tracked down by police and charged with fraud, arson and improperly interfering with a dead body.

So it would seem that restless spirits, as well as the souls of those at rest, are in copious supply at Waikumete. And the ghost stories that have collected over the years are legion. The chapel has its own resident ghost, a black-clad woman observed either peering balefully out of the window or drifting through the grounds outside. This apparition is usually seen by cemetery workers more often than mourners, and is believed to be the spirit of a former sexton's wife returning to check on their work.

Arthur Smith, a man who worked in the cemetery's crematorium for years (and does not get spooked easily) was once terrified by a female apparition as he was locking up and heading home from work one day:

It was a clear day. I'd just turned to open the door of my car, which was facing the road ahead, when lo and behold, standing in the middle of the road, there was a lady in bare feet with a long type of gown on. It was a sort of off-white colour. Her hair was unkempt. But what disturbed me most was her gaze, which was fixed firmly on me. She wouldn't stop looking at me. I thought to myself: just get in your car, don't look at her, drive through the gate, get out, shut it and get back in your car and out of there as quick as you can. When I reached the gate and got out I looked back, but she had gone, as though she had disappeared into thin air. I had never seen that lady before. I have never seen her since. It is something I have lived with all my life. I have never forgotten it and never will.

Mary Gilligan, a member of the Friends of Waikumete Group that hold regular tours of the cemetery, has seen the apparition of a white-clad lady in the cemetery. Her encounter occurred early one morning while taking her dog for a walk. On another occasion, she witnessed a tall figure wearing a long robe and a wide-brimmed hat flitting between graves. Both sightings occurred in the old section of the cemetery.

The old section is rambling and rundown, the pathways uneven and overgrown. The deeper one descends into this section, the older and more unkempt the graves get — most of them crumbling, some beyond recognition — until they seem to disappear altogether into a thicket of forest at the base of a steep gully.

One grave of particular significance in this part of the cemetery is that of Alexander McFarlane, who is associated with one of the most unsettling local haunting tales. His ghost is not so much associated with the cemetery itself, but up the hill on the platform of Glen Eden railway station. McFarlane was a tablet porter at the station during the 1920s and lived adjacent to the cemetery. He was considered something of a practical joker, renowned locally for a prank he once played on a Jamaican immigrant, Darky Saunders. The McFarlanes would occasionally invite Darky into their home for a meal, although he tended to outstay his welcome. One night the family saw him coming and pretended not to be at home. After tiring of knocking, Darky wandered off to lie in the grass between the McFarlane house and the cemetery gate, presumably to await their return. He fell asleep, and McFarlane hatched a plan to scare him off, hollowing out a pumpkin and carving a face in it, Halloween-style. He then inserted a candle and slung it over the cemetery fence, hiding behind the fence, groaning and rattling a chain. Darky woke from his slumber, bolted in fright, and was not seen for ages. When McFarlane later bumped into the Jamaican, a wide-eyed Darky related how an evil spirit had come after him out of the cemetery.

Ironically McFarlane, the committed prankster, survived both the First World War and the Spanish influenza epidemic, only to be struck down by a freak industrial accident at his place of work. Back in those days it was not uncommon for mailbags awaiting transport by train to be slung over the edge of the platform by a rather ingenious contraption. Rather than having to come to a complete stop to pick up the mail, a train would merely have to slow down, whereupon a mail hook would swing into position and collect the mail bag so the train could continue on its way. One fateful day the mail hook caught McFarlane off guard — he was struck between the eyes by it and instantly killed. His grave is a stone's throw from where the accident occurred.

Over the years, tales grew of the ghostly porter who was regularly spotted standing alone at one end of the platform as though waiting for the mail. Reports have been less frequent in recent years, largely due to the fact that Glen Eden railway station was relocated to the centre of town. The platform where McFarlane met his gruesome demise is now disused and surrounded by the industrial estate. However, stories still filter through of a solitary figure, in what appears to be a period porter uniform, glimpsed by commuters from the train as they rattle past the abandoned site.

More curious still are accounts of haunting on the site of the new Glen Eden railway station, attributed to the fact that the historic station house was moved to the new location. This is the station house that McFarlane worked from, and where coffins were stored before final transportation into the cemetery. Today it houses the Platform 7 café, where strange goings on are continually reported by staff: items are tossed onto the kitchen floor while their backs are turned; ovens turn themselves on and off; ghostly faces are seen staring in through the window. Keri Clarke, a former employee of the café, recalls a chilling encounter on her very first day of work:

> We hadn't open up yet and the door was shut. I remember I was bending down behind the counter, and when I looked up there was a man standing in front of me. I hadn't heard him walk in. And I didn't hear the door, which was still shut. I told him that we weren't open for business yet, and perhaps he'd like to come back in half an hour. He was dressed in very old-fashioned clothing and wore an old-style hat, which I thought was kind of strange ... He then asked me if I knew when the next train would be coming. I told him there was a timetable outside on the platform. He thanked me, and instead of heading outside he

turned around to study the framed historic timetable we have displayed on the wall. I was feeling a bit uncomfortable, so I stepped into the kitchen, which is just a few steps away. When I looked back a moment later, he had disappeared. Without a sound. No footsteps. No door opening and closing.

Was this the ghost of Alexander McFarlane? Keri thinks otherwise. The figure she saw was certainly in period garb, but not a uniform. She believes it could have been the spirit of any one of the many souls whose casket spent time at the Glen Eden railway station. Nevertheless, children especially continue to claim to have seen a tall, bearded figure wearing a grey trench coat and dressed in an 'olden days uniform' standing solemnly on the platform ...

THE *GHOST HUNT* FILES

As the *Ghost Hunt* team arrived to set up in Waikumete Cemetery on a bright blue afternoon, Carolyn was the first to admit a feeling of unease: 'You just hear so many stories of graveyards containing spirits with unfinished business. Maybe they don't actually know they're dead, and that's why they're still wandering.' Michael noted the dichotomous nature of the enormous graveyard: 'It's an interesting mixture of a place that's really eerie but also a place that's really peaceful.' Team leader Brad was concerned about the logistics of the investigation. Area-wise, this would be the largest ghost hunt the team would launch. Initially gung-ho about the enterprise, he was somewhat taken aback by the dilapidated state of the old section of the cemetery: 'Seeing it so overrun really kicks the point home — it's all about death and this is what it looks like.'

Brad opted to focus the operation on the current station platform, where Keri Clarke had her encounter, and, logically enough, in the older section of the cemetery. It was during early twilight, when setting up surveillance equipment on the edge of the gully near this section, that Brad had a bizarre experience of his own. A groaning sound was clearly audible, which was determined not to be wind (it was a perfectly still evening), and too close to earshot to have been attributable to the distant rumble of traffic. Brad heard the disturbing noise repeatedly as he ventured around the site, so many times that he was prompted to click off a few photographs in the murky semi-darkness.

When analysed later, one of these shots reveal what appear to be the blurred silhouette of a human figure, perched between two gravestones and wearing a cap. Comparing this

Alexander McFarlane, a former tablet porter at nearby Glen Eden railway station, is himself buried at Waikumete near to where this cap-wearing apparition was photographed.

to photographs taken in the same location during daylight reveals nothing to account for the anomaly — the space between the headstones should be completely vacant. The cap and the close proximity to Alexander McFarlane's grave begged the obvious question: Could this be his apparition? Brad was uncertain why the spirit would manifest itself in the cemetery on this particular occasion, when it was previously known only to appear on the station platform. But, as he rightly asserted, in the realm of ghost hunting the only certainty is that *nothing* is certain.

The cloudless afternoon gave way to a cloudless night and a full moon that cast a spectral glow on the whole cemetery. Michael began his investigation by heading across the patch of ground where the victims of the Spanish influenza are buried, and into the heavily wooded Murderers' Grove. From there, he headed deep into the heart of the old section of the cemetery. Although sensing no presences anywhere, his photographic efforts bore fruit. One shot, taken near the beginning of his trek, reveals a plethora of orbs rising up from the graveyard ground. Indiscernible to the human eye, they were picked up by Michael's camera owing to its light-sensitive setting. Carolyn was particularly astounded by the shot: 'It's like the souls of 1600 have come up to visit!' Yet another photograph revealed a single bright blue orb, floating in mid-air. Paranormal experts believe such vivid coloration reflects a high intensity of spiritual energy.

A mysterious event transpired as Carolyn investigated the railway station. Brad had been inside the café earlier in the evening setting up equipment, and observed that the café proprietor had deactivated the security alarm system. Yet

Michael's photographs revealed orbs rising or hovering close to the ground in the cemetery — the range of orb colours reflects the intensity of paranormal energy.

as Carolyn entered in the dark, the alarm began to sound! Fortuitously, a surveillance camera had been pointed in the direction of the alarm console, and on replaying the video footage, the alarm console is seen to be re-arming itself, moments before Carolyn's entrance — as though the buttons were being pushed by invisible spectral fingers ...

Perhaps they belonged to the phantom face that was captured on videotape only minutes later, passing by and peering in the kitchen window, just after Carolyn stepped out of the room. The translucent visage is apparent only for a few frames, but it possesses distinct human features. Exterior cameras set up on the same angle reveal not a living soul, but an empty platform. Could this have been the spirit of Alexander McFarlane, practical joker, playing a prank from the other side? The *Ghost Hunt* team were left with no uncertainty that both Waikumete Cemetery and the Glen Eden railway station are exceptionally haunted sites.

9. st james theatre, wellington

Theatres are notoriously haunted buildings — there are very few in the world that do *not* lay claim to at least one resident spirit. The Theatre Royal in London's Drury Lane alone boasts over 500 alleged ghosts! New Zealand's theatres are certainly not immune to ghostly phenomena, and nearly every theatre is occupied by a past actor, stagehand or theatre manager doomed to tread the boards for eternity.

Theatres are places of enormous energy, melodrama, laughter, tears and expression — a space filled with compressed human feelings. Every gamut of emotion is played out nightly by its actors, many throwing themselves into their performance with extremes of passion. If the actors do their job properly, the audience is also affected by the performance, laughing or crying along with the players and adding to the emotional atmosphere. If ghosts or spirits react to this highly charged energy, it is little wonder they linger well after the curtains have closed.

Actors tend to be intensely creative individuals, enjoying the spotlight and demanding attention, and many alleged theatre ghosts are said to be the spirits of actors who either succeeded or failed on that particular stage. It seems that even a literal death cannot stop some actors wanting the spotlight, their ghosts either spending eternity enjoying the kudos of a good review or reliving a mortifying 'death' on stage. The majority of theatres have a ghost that the actors attribute omens to, and the sighting of a particular ghost can either herald success or doom the production to failure.

Superstition abounds in the world of the theatre: before going on stage actors are advised to 'break a leg' — a warped way of wishing a performer good luck; green is considered an unlucky colour — despite the fact that the actors' offstage waiting room is known as the Green Room; and, of course, no actor in their right mind will mention Shakespeare's 'Scottish play' by name ...

Teams of carpenters, electricians, set designers and artists transform the theatre interior with each production, and it is said that this intense activity may trigger ghost sightings. The constant building work associated with theatres has been attributed to increased paranormal activity.

Haunted theatres in New Zealand

A simple Internet search reveals an extraordinary number of haunted theatres around the world. New Zealand is no exception, and nearly every stage — from large city venues to small community stages — boasts a supernatural mascot or two.

The opulent Civic Theatre in Auckland, with its lavish oriental-themed interior, is haunted by the ghost of its former manager, Colin Anderson, who committed suicide in the 1930s after a love affair went horribly wrong.

There have been many other sightings of 'Man in a Grey Suit' in various parts of the theatre.

The Hawke's Bay Opera House in Hastings Street has at least four reputed ghosts: an active, playful spirit haunts the fly floor, said to be a flyman of a touring ballet company who fell to his death; a woman in a red dress lives in a side stairwell — it is said that she has a penchant for other women and follows them around before and after performances; the ghost of a small child; and the spirit of an elderly, grey-haired gentleman, all seen by staff and even entire audiences.

Down the road from the St James, the Wellington Opera House is haunted by the spirit of its architect, Albert Liddy, who committed suicide in the design office at the rear of the theatre. It is said that accidents befall anyone who dares criticise his creation. The Hannah Playhouse, also in Courtenay Place, is haunted by a worker who fell to his death during its construction in 1973.

The Royal Wanganui Opera House features an icy presence known as Frank, a cranky spirit who seems to object to excessive sound levels during some concerts. Frank is said to be the former manager of the Opera House, who collapsed and died backstage during a performance in the late 1950s.

The haunted underground stream of Dunedin that runs beneath the Fortune Theatre [see chapter 4] also runs beneath the Regent, the site of a fatal 1879 fire that killed 12 people. Naturally, this is a place of intense paranormal activity.

Most of the country's grand theatres including the Civic in Auckland, the Wellington Opera House, the Hawke's Bay Opera House and the wooden Theatre Royal in Nelson boast at least one resident spook. Arguably, the best-documented theatre ghost stories come from one of the most ornate stages in the country, Wellington's St James Theatre. This beautiful performing arts theatre, located in the heart of Courtenay Place in New Zealand's capital, was built in 1912, incidentally (and perhaps, significantly) on the site of an old graveyard. Originally known as His Majesty's Theatre, it was the largest vaudeville and picture theatre in Australasia, and the first to be constructed from reinforced concrete and steel.

Architect Henry White designed the St James theatre to be lower and broader than usual to encourage more emotional intimacy between the actors and audience.

1/1-015972; F. Alexander Turnbull Library, Wellington.

Its architect, Henry White, was a skilled engineer who designed 120 theatres in the southern hemisphere, including the Hawke's Bay Opera House, the Plaza in Christchurch and the Capitol Theatre in Sydney. A perfectionist, White insisted that the St James be lower and broader than normal to allow greater intimacy between the actors and the audience. It is said that, before construction, he built a scale model of the theatre, stretching a string of cotton between every seat and the stage to ensure that every patron had a perfect view of the stage.

To describe the interior of the St James as lavish is an understatement. It is ornately decorated with elaborate cherubim, plaster curlicues and gilded masks representing comedy, drama and opera; it features three tiers of seating, complete with balcony boxes draped in plush red velvet; and a red and gold stage curtain sits above the enormous performance space, which is flanked by flies that soar 15 metres above the stage.

Despite its magnificence, the old building has had a chequered past. Originally built to showcase vaudeville performances, it was forced to change with the times and popular taste, transforming into a cinema in the 1920s. With the advent of television some thirty years later, however, cinema also went into a slump and the St James fell into disrepair. Although recognised as a building of special significance, the St James Theatre was earmarked for demolition in the mid-1980s. But the people of Wellington refused to let this treasure be destroyed, and after a massive community protest the theatre was given a reprieve, undergoing refurbishment at a cost of nearly $20 million.

The rejuvenated St James now provides a home for the Royal New Zealand Ballet, offering the best stage for dance in the country. It also showcases large theatrical productions and musical events. The theatre is now recognised by New Zealand Historic Places Trust as a Category 1 building of 'special and outstanding cultural and historical significance'.

With its place in Wellington's cultural life secure, it seems the spirits who dwell in this theatre have a permanent home. According to local historian and author David McGill, there is a plethora of ghosts inhabiting the St James including a ghost cat, the spirit of a limping, asthmatic stage manager, the ghost of the architect Henry White and an entire boys' choir.

Weathering its transformation into a movie cinema in the 1920s, and saved from demolition in the 1980s by the people of Wellington, the St James Theatre has been lovingly restored to its original state including sculptured cherubim and plaster curlicues.

These ghost stories date back to its days as a vaudeville theatre, although most of the sightings took place during its years as a cinema. In his book *Full Circle: The History of the St James Theatre* (1998), David McGill interviewed many cinema staff members, all of whom recounted vivid tales of ghostly encounters.

> The stories just lingered on, even though it wasn't a theatre any more. These were ordinary people who sold sweets in the store, ran the projection, people who didn't have any interest in ghosts. But all of them would tell stories to me about the ghosts ... They all knew the history, but nobody could tell me how they knew it. It's oral history, passed on through word of mouth. They may not be in the official channels of a city, but in the underground area where people gossip, the stories linger on.

One of the most chilling stories David recounts in his book was from the 1970s, when the police were called into the theatre to investigate claims of fold-down seats slamming shut by themselves in the gallery. The police dogs sent up to investigate refused to enter the gallery:

> The hackles rose on the back of their necks. Something frightened them, and they wouldn't go into that area to investigate.

According to David, the dogs were possibly reacting to the presence of a nasty, somewhat vengeful entity known as the Wailing Woman. She was an actress who performed at some point at the St James, but was booed off stage after a bad performance. After retiring to her dressing room, she committed suicide by slashing her wrists. David says:

When violent deeds happen, ghosts seem to linger on. The Wailing Woman is not at peace. But she does have an attachment to the place where she tried to make her name or impress people.

In *Full Circle*, David tells the story of a former caretaker, Bob Hesketh, who had a run-in with the Wailing Woman:

A few days later he was in the staffroom at 11 a.m. when he heard a wailing sound. He rushed out. The sound was coming from the auditorium. The door was locked. There was nobody inside. Nina the usherette and Jean the cashier told him it was the Wailing Woman, a vaudevillian actress who had tried to make a comeback, was booed off stage, went home and slit her wrists. They had heard her wailing a number of times … (p. 55)

Another two staff members recalled seeing a woman in a red dress running through the flooded basement after pipes malfunctioned. According to theatre lore, the Wailing Woman is responsible for some of the physical misfortunes that have occurred in the theatre, such as actors spraining ankles, injuring themselves before a performance or catching a bad dose of flu. David himself claims that, during one of his interviews with the cinema staff, he saw a shadowy figure in the gallery that may well have been the Wailing Woman:

I was taken by torchlight into dark old areas where no one ever came then. It wasn't plush like now. The projectionist was talking about the Wailing Woman, and then we saw a movement and felt a chill. I don't know if it's the power of suggestion — I didn't come here looking for a ghost story, because before that I didn't know about it.

The most infamous of all the St James' ghosts is Yuri, a Russian ballet dancer who either fell or was pushed to his death from the flies during the theatre's early days. Described as a shadowy figure wearing a black cloak or a coat, possibly an opera cloak, Yuri's apparition has been seen on a number of occasions by various staff members over the years and

Soaring 15 metres above the stage, the flies have been the location of many paranormal close encounters.

Famous theatre ghosts

Among the countless spirits haunting theatres around the world, there are also many 'celebrity' ghosts — famous actors and playwrights who eternally linger on their favourite stages.

The Princess Theatre in Melbourne, Australia, is haunted by the ghost of Federici, who died on stage in 1888 while performing the part of Mephistopheles in the opera *Faust*. Apparently the singer suffered a heart attack as he descended into 'hell' via an on-stage trapdoor. Since that time, dozens of actors (including 70 percent of the cast of *Les Miserables*), theatre workers and audience members have witnessed this real-life 'phantom of the opera'.

The ghost of actor Victor Killian is said to roam the sidewalk outside Mann's Chinese Theatre, Los Angeles, searching for the man who murdered him there in 1982. Meanwhile at the Pantages Theatre, elsewhere in Los Angeles, the cigarette-smoking ghost of a tall, thin man, rumoured to be the spirit of eccentric millionaire Howard Hughes, haunts the offices.

Welsh author and poet, Dylan Thomas, has chosen to spend eternity in the corridors of the Bush Theatre in London's Shepherd's Bush. Thomas apparently worked for the BBC when the theatre was a rehearsal room for BBC Radio.

The disembodied head of the famous clown, Joseph Grimaldi, has been seen both at Drury Lane Theatre, London, and also at Sadler's Wells Theatre, Islington, where he appears in full clown make-up behind audience members sitting in one of the boxes. Considering the clown died of natural causes in his home, one can only assume that he's on an eternal search for entertainment in these theatres!

Wit and raconteur George Bernard Shaw is said to haunt the Festival Theatre in Malvern, England, while famous French actress Sarah Bernhardt wanders the stage of the Theatre Royal, Brighton.

Another gruesome apparition is that of illusionist Sigmund Neuberger, who burned to death in the fire of 1892 at the Empire Palace Theatre, Edinburgh. While that particular theatre has been demolished, Neuberger's ghost still lingers at the Edinburgh Festival Theatre, which today stands on the site of the tragedy.

nearly everyone at the theatre can attest that the flies possess an eerie, chilling ambience — some say they always feel watched as they descend from its rickety heights.

According to theatre staff, Yuri is a prankster, taunting cast members and staff with flashing lights, removing light bulbs, closing curtains, slamming seats and setting false fire alarms. But he is also known as a helpful ghost, even saving lives. *Full Circle* recounts the story of a former projectionist, Jim Hutchison, who claims that Yuri saved the lives of him and his family on two separate occasions in the 1960s:

I was dressing the stage late one night. About midnight, I was up on the fly floor and about to head back down when the lights went out. I knew the area pretty well and though I was by the safety rail, beside the ladder, I felt this very strong feeling of being pushed backwards, and this intense cold, like I had a packet of frozen peas on my chest. I looked closely where I was about to step. There was a drop of 10 metres … (p. 58)

On another occasion, Mr Hutchison's wife and their eight-month-old baby were pushed from the path of a falling set beam by invisible hands — perhaps by Yuri's helpful spirit? A seance held at the theatre in the seventies revealed that Yuri was pushed to his death by a woman called Pasha, although no one has yet confirmed this story's historic credence.

Another of St James' ghostly residents is the spirit of Stan Andrews, a former theatre manager who died in 1965. Many claim to have heard Stan, an asthmatic who limped, coming up behind them — a ghostly wheeze accompanied by a shuffling footfall …

Then there are disembodied angelic voices that can be heard wafting through the theatre from time to time, perhaps the voices of the boys' choir who performed at the St James just before the Second World War, before setting sail on an overseas cruise, never to be seen again …

Since the St James Theatre has been renovated, there have been fewer and fewer ghost sightings, although Yuri still seems to lend a helping hand occasionally. Perhaps the restless spirits are finally appeased now that this magnificent building is being used to its full potential and regarded with the respect it deserves.

THE *GHOST HUNT* FILES

Unlike Dunedin's Fortune Theatre (see chapter 4), which is a prop-filled rabbit warren with a busy, lived-in ambience, the St James Theatre is cavernous. It feels very much like an empty shell waiting to be filled, and between productions this is exactly what it is – the props rooms lie empty, dressing rooms bare, corridors stark and cold. Front of house, the curtain is raised to reveal a huge, barren stage. The plush auditorium seats are all neatly shut, aisles clear and the cherubim, gargoyles and Greek-style torsos stare out into a void, as if the gods themselves are waiting for the show to begin.

Arriving at the St James for the *Ghost Hunt* was an uncomfortable experience for Carolyn. In the past she has watched numerous productions at the theatre and these had always been joyous occasions. To see it in its pre-show state disconcerted her, knowing that later that night she would be wandering through its dark interior. Michael, on the other hand, was in his element, strutting around on stage and rehearsing a monologue. He was looking forward to investigating the rumours of hauntings, and was particularly keen to search for the ghost of the Russian ballet dancer, Yuri.

As Brad was setting up his camera equipment, he had a strange experience that recalled Yuri's reputation as a prankster. He had just finished securing a camera tripod to the floor in the stairwell, returning to the area after only five minutes to find the camera broken into two pieces at the bottom on the stairs. No one had been in the area and the tripod had been securely fastened ... was it Yuri demanding that our team leave? Or was he just taunting Brad in his typical playful manner? Undeterred, Brad sent the two investigators off into the dark: Michael to the stage and the auditorium; Carolyn into the flies above the stage, and then down under the orchestra pit.

Carolyn was immediately jumpy, thrown by the impenetrable darkness and the rickety heights of the metal flies. Strange noises emanating from behind set her nerves on edge. Hovering high above the stage, Carolyn empathised with Yuri's vulnerability. She asked Yuri's permission before snapping off a photo into the darkness. On descending to the first floor, Brad directed her to the dressing room where the Wailing Woman was rumoured to have committed suicide. Although Carolyn felt a considerable temperature drop while inside this room, the only thing that really scared her was seeing her own reflection in the bank of mirrors! On exiting the dressing room, however, a sequence of strange events began to take place: firstly, Carolyn could hear the elevator moving on its own even though she had yet to call it; secondly, she heard noises coming from the empty stairwell below her. As her fears mounted, Brad saw something even more bizarre on his surveillance cameras — a round orb, floating rapidly down the corridor where Carolyn had just been, travelling straight towards the camera before disappearing off-screen.

Sensing Carolyn's anxiety, Brad advised her to quickly get into the waiting elevator, but her uncertainty about what (or who) could be inside prevented her from doing so. Finally, the elevator doors opened and Carolyn stepped inside to send it towards the basement ... only to have the doors close behind her, trapping her inside.

After exploring the stage, Michael headed up the creaky stairwell into the area known as the Gods, the uppermost level of theatre seating. This is an area renowned for paranormal activity — and where the police dogs' hackles rose in fear and they refused to enter during their earlier investigation. Michael's explorations were interrupted by an alarm registering on Brad's surveillance system. A barometer set up in an archive room had peaked, indicating a paranormal intruder. Brad directed Michael to the room, located in a cellar area. The dingy room, dank and cold, was an unpleasant environment even for Michael. The alarm was making a continual beeping noise, and Michael took several photos as evidence.

Carolyn was also called upon to check the levels on one of Brad's trifield meters, placed under the stage. She bid a hasty retreat from the area, however, claiming that the area 'felt like a coffin'. She did pluck up the courage to take some photos, which revealed an impressive number of orbs clustered around the stage area.

Michael's photo taken in the gallery also exposed an unusually high number of orbs of differing sizes, indicating a great deal of spiritual activity in the theatre that night. This evidence, while not definitive proof of a paranormal presence, serves as an effective backup to other material collected during the investigation. Considering Brad recorded an orb, in flight, on his computer system, and two alarms registered changing temperature and electromagnetic field levels, the photographs only serve to confirm what was felt by the team during their nocturnal investigation.

It was the photo taken by Carolyn in the flies, however,

An unusually high number of orbs detected in the theatre, while in themselves not conclusive evidence of a paranormal presence, reinforced the findings of the investigation.

The intriguing black form (centre frame) could be the apparition of Yuri, a Russian ballet dancer who fell to his death from the flies in the theatre's very early years.

that was truly telling. Taken in pitch darkness, the photograph captured the edge of the railing and a ceiling beam, flaring in the light of the flash. But as Brad lightened the photo an intriguing black shape is revealed — an elongated figure, suspended in mid-air. An optical illusion, perhaps, or the apparition of Yuri falling to his death?

10. ewelme cottage and kinder house, parnell, auckland

Spooky occurrences even happen in one of the most fashionable suburbs of Auckland. Ayr Street, Parnell, is the location of two historic and reputedly haunted houses. Kinder House, now an art gallery, is the former home of the Church of England reverend, teacher, painter and photographer John Kinder, and is haunted by the apparition of a man clad in black. Just metres away is Ewelme Cottage, built in 1863 for another Church of England clergyman, the Reverend Vicesimus Lush, his wife Blanche and their six children. Ewelme Cottage, best known for its starring role in the Oscar-winning film *The Piano*, is the regular haunt of several ghosts, all of them the spirits of women and children.

Paranormal activity occurring in two separate buildings just down the road from each other comes as little surprise considering the shared history of the homes. The Kinder and Lush families were close friends as well as neighbours. The Lush children attended Auckland Grammar School when it was presided over by the Reverend Kinder.

Aesthetically, the houses could not be more different. Kinder House is an austere, Gothic-style, double-storey mansion built from grey stone that was quarried from Mt Eden. Ewelme Cottage, on the other hand, is a picture-postcard, weatherboard cottage, warm and inviting, furnished with antique family heirlooms and surrounded by award-winning gardens. Ewelme exudes a serene, feminine gentility whereas Kinder House has a masculine, sober and serious ambience.

Ewelme Cottage was continuously occupied by the Lush family until 1968, and it retains its cosy and lived-in atmosphere. Walking into Ewelme Cottage is like entering a time warp — one easily imagines the laughter of children, the clink of family dinners being prepared in the original kitchen and the tinkle of the piano being played in the drawing room. Preserved as a house museum, it has been left exactly as it was when the Lush family bequeathed it to the New Zealand Historic Places Trust in 1969, complete with old books, letters, diaries and family photographs. The atmosphere is typical of an Auckland middle-class family in the Victorian era, with furnishings and an artwork collection gathered for over a century.

Built in 1863, Ewelme Cottage is one of several haunted historic homes found in Auckland.

Haunted Ayr Street

Ayr Street, Parnell has had a reputation for spooky happenings since 1901, when a newspaper report from the *New Zealand Herald* stated that a ghost was terrifying locals and making women swoon in fear. The so-called ghost was seen in several places, one of which was Ayr Street. As it turned out, it was just a naughty local teenager dressed up in a sheet!

The street also gained notoriety during the 1960s when the body of a young boy was found buried beneath a house. The boy, lured from a hotel in Carlton Gore Road, had been sexually abused before being brutally slain. The house where this tragedy occurred has since been demolished.

According to the curator of Ewelme Cottage, John Webster, the cottage resounds with the memories and spirits of the Lush family. John has curated the house since 1973 and lived on the premises for 22 years, during which time he has seen and heard many things that lead him to believe that the place is haunted:

> *I have personally seen female spirits, and I've even seen things like cupboard doors opening and closing. We also have a ghost cat, which was here before me — the Lushes were great cat lovers. I have also heard noises, the sound of talking in the hallway. That happened at night, but all the other apparitions were seen in the daytime. The idea that ghostly apparitions only happen at night certainly doesn't happen here.*

Despite his many experiences, John is yet to witness the most commonly seen manifestation at Ewelme Cottage — the spirit of a young girl:

> *She is described as blonde, with ringlets in her hair, possibly wearing a white dress and a blue sash. The latest sightings of that came from two children in 2004; both these children came from upstairs and mentioned that they had been playing with a young girl. She has also been seen under the oak tree in the garden, and she has even been photographed there.*

Despite his intimate knowledge of the Lush family history, John says that the identity of this ghost-child remains a mystery. There are no reported deaths of children in the house, and although three of the Lush children died of scarlet fever that event occurred in 1864 before the family lived in the house. The physical aspect of the alleged ghost does, however, resemble one of these children, Eliza. John speculates that her spirit may have followed her family to their warm and loving home.

Whoever the spirit may be it is obvious that it is a child who was attached to the house and refuses to leave her place of refuge. According to John, sightings of the Ewelme ghosts date back to 1945, when one of the Lush descendants, Aroha Lush Ruddock, wrote a poem about the house. This young woman had led a troubled life and was regularly in hospital suffering with psychological problems. As part of her therapy she composed four verses about the house, one of which alludes to the magnificent oak tree in the garden:

The oak tree in Ewelme's garden is where the ghost-child, identity unknown, has been appearing to visitors since 1945.

And when the stars and moon shine bright
Gay child ghosts play around the tree
They who now have passed our sight
And so are spirit sweetly free.

Local clairvoyant Justine O'Gahdra-Sharp believes the ghost-child may well be the spirit of the talented young poet herself, a young woman who had periods of great anguish as she coped with her mental problems. According to Justine, the far room of the attic emanates with the troubled soul of this young woman, with great feelings of distress and claustrophobia, as if the woman had been locked in the room:

I could hear crying, and a sensation of hopelessness. I heard her
say to me that she felt unloved and abandoned, that she was
all alone. I also noticed that the door lock had been broken, that
she was definitely locked in that room. When she was put in that
room, it was not of her own volition.

John Webster verifies this, as it is likely that the young woman was locked in the room or restrained there during fits of insanity.

Climbing the narrow staircase to the attic one becomes aware that this was at one time a child's environment. This is where the Lush children and grandchildren slept and played.

Each of the three rooms upstairs has had its own ghostly visitations: John has witnessed the figure of a woman in the right-hand bedroom, while the ghost-child has been seen in the other rooms, usually by other children visiting the house.

The house has a totally different feel downstairs — more adult and sophisticated. According to Justine, the study has a

The study at Ewelme Cottage is fitted with original furnishings belonging to William Lush, son of the Reverend Vicesimus Lush.

very male energy, which makes sense considering the room is overflowing with old books and personal items belonging to William Edward Lush, the son of Vicesimus. The ghost-child has also been sighted in this room, hiding behind the chair in the far corner.

The drawing room, which has French doors opening onto the verandah, is where several people report seeing the ghost of a small woman. During ghost tours, held by John Webster several years ago, candles in this room would, on a regular basis, either refuse to light or mysteriously blow out on their own ... perhaps the pranks of a playful spirit?

Perhaps the most disturbing supernatural phenomenon at Ewelme Cottage occurred one night as John was walking through the hallway. He heard 'otherworldly voices', one male, one female, in conversation:

> *Initially I thought I'd left the radio on, or a window was open and I was picking up someone else's noise, but then I realised it was suspended in mid-air, in the hallway, under the light. It appeared to be two distinct tones of voice. One was a light one, the other was deeper. I couldn't make out the words, but I would have liked to have heard what they were talking about.*

The phenomenon of voices beyond the grave is a fascinating, seldom-explored area, though one which has been attracting its share of attention in paranormal circles since the release of the Hollywood movie *White Noise* in 2005. The theory holds that intelligible voices can be recorded on electronic instruments such as tape recorders and television sets, capturing information recorded into the fabric of the physical world. This phenomenon is called EVP (Electronic Voice Phenomenon).

The ability to hear and sense voices and sounds from the past is known as clairaudience, and is a rare gift possessed by Justine O'Gahdra-Sharp. Communicating with the spirit world like this is not always straightforward:

> *Clairaudient is when you hear things, basically, you receive messages. It's like a feeling, but you can also hear laughter or crying or certain words. Clairvoyant is very much the visual … When I'm asked to give a reading of a place, first of all I have to centre myself and connect with the energy of the place, either by burning incense or with crystals. Then I try to get a sense of the history, what energies or emotions that may have left an impression of the place. I see imagery and photographs in my mind, and I sometimes hear these characters talking to me.*

At Kinder House, Justine immediately sensed the presence of dominant male forces, driving the day-to-day dramas and workings of the home. This fits with the image of John Kinder, a man described as stern, with 'little sense of humour and little tolerance for those who disagreed with him on theological matters'. Born in London in 1819, he was educated at Cambridge University before entering the Anglican ministry. In 1855 he emigrated to Auckland where he was appointed Headmaster of the Church of England Grammar School from 1855 to 1872. The school was located across the road from the large grey mansion built for Kinder.

As well as being a theologian and academic, the balding, bearded Kinder was an artist and photographer of note. His watercolours of New Zealand's dramatic landscapes, particularly the images of the Pink and White Terraces at Rotorua prior to the eruption of Mt Tarawera in 1886, are now world famous and have elevated his position among New Zealand's most important artists. Today, his achievements as an artist far outweigh his pursuits in education and ecclesiology. Kinder married Marianne Celia Brown. They had no children of their own, however, in 1866 they adopted the children of John's brother Henry, who had died under tragic circumstances.

Therein lies the mystery behind the haunting at Kinder House. According to John Webster, who reports seeing a shadowy, black-clad apparition disappearing up the stairs, the ghost is most likely that of John Kinder himself, a man who, in life, was very attached to the house. Others believe that the ghost is actually Henry, the brother who was murdered by his wife and her lover.

EVP

The concept of recording voices from beyond the grave dates back to 1959, when a Swedish researcher, Friedrich Juergenson, discovered mysterious voices in the background of his bird song recordings. After first thinking his tape recorder was defective, Friedrich realised that an invisible intelligence was addressing him by name and trying to establish contact with him.

Then in 1971 a Latvian scientist, Dr Konstantine Raudive, applied the principle that background noise acts as a carrier and can be modulated by other signals present in space. Without background noise, these signals are too weak to be detectable, but in the presence of 'white noise', or tape hiss, their levels increase and can be heard by the human ear.

It is generally accepted that the human voice is incapable of speaking below 280 Hz. Most EVP (Electronic Voice Phenomenon) sound recordings are captured between 30 and 300 Hz, a level that it is impossible for the human voice to emit.

To test the theory of EVP at Ewelme Cottage, a vintage high quality professional recording unit called a Nagra was set up, the type of device once used to record sounds on feature films. This is an analogue recording device, believed by some to give a more accurate sound recording than a modern, digital recorder.

By recording at double speed and at a high level, the extremely sensitive microphone picks up ambient sounds humans could never hear with the naked ear, sounds which are all around us but beyond the decibel range of our hearing. The benefits of this increased sensitivity is that you can hear more, but the downside is the increase in background distortion, generally known as white noise.

The results of the audio experiment conducted by the *Ghost Hunt* team at Ewelme Cottage were intriguing. Recording throughout the night at extremely high levels, most of the recording is simply static — atmospheric noises distorted by a disconcerting hiss. By feeding the recording through an audio program on a computer, however, the investigators were able to equalise the tape hiss and remove the lower registers, cleaning up the recording and revealing fascinating anomalies.

At one particular moment during the evening, ironically enough at exactly the same time Michael was attempting to commune with the spirit of the young girl in the attic, a faint child-like voice can vaguely be detected. By removing even more of the frequencies below 280 Hz and thereby reducing the noise, this voice becomes more distinct. Disturbingly, the investigators believed they could hear the words 'go away' ...

Whether this voice was, in fact, the sound of a child communicating from the other side, or simply an aberration on the tape, or an electronic anomaly sent via sound waves, we may never know, but it lends weight to the theory that the dead can communicate with others in the physical world.

Henry was, according to John Webster, a colourful local character, and his demise was one of the biggest scandals to hit Auckland society in the mid-nineteenth century. Known as a heavy drinker, his name became linked to embezzlement and bank fraud. To escape prying eyes and the inevitable gossip, Henry and his wife Maria Ellen and her parents, moved to Sydney in 1864 with their two children, Harry and Nesta. Tragedy struck the following year, however, when the body of Henry was found floating in Sydney Harbour — the victim, so it seemed, of suicide. It soon emerged that Henry had been poisoned with laudanum and then shot. Even worse, the heinous crime had been orchestrated by Ellen and her lover, a Sydney dentist. The dentist was charged with murder, but although Ellen was acquitted she was 'no longer considered a suitable parent' and the children returned to Auckland where they were adopted by their Uncle John.

Despite John Webster's protestations that the spirit haunting Kinder House could not possibly be Henry — as Henry had never inhabited the house — on first walking into the house and with no prior knowledge of the family history, Justine immediately sensed the presence of 'a man with a moustache, possibly a banker or involved with banks.' She could 'hear gunfire, and there was poison involved ... and it's all revolving around an affair.' In addition, Justine sensed the presence of two children, '... a young boy, and a girl with serious eyes'. This fits the image of the two Kinder children who were brought up as John and Celia's own. Celia herself described the children in letters as 'nice little mortals, considering all things — the great trouble is that they are regular little rips'.

Many of Justine's initial impressions about both Kinder House and Ewelme Cottage were eventually corroborated with historic evidence. This supports the theory that old houses hold on to the energies of the past, and that a family history and connection to a house can continue beyond the earthly plane. In the case of Ewelme Cottage, the old books, photos and furniture immediately transport visitors back to another era, while John Kinder's comprehensive art collection offers a view of New Zealand in the nineteenth century.

In paranormal terms the energy of the past is known as 'spiritual residue' (see chapter 1), trace energy that has been left behind which suggests the emotional tone and history of a place. In other words, the inhabitants of the houses, particularly those with stronger attachment to the place, leave behind their psychic imprint on the physical environment. Both houses reveal so much about their former owners, but it seems that they also have secrets they are not quite ready to reveal, such as the identity of the shadowy apparitions that haunt their corridors.

THE *GHOST HUNT* FILES

The vastly different energies of the two neighbouring properties was evident from the moment the *Ghost Hunt* team arrived in Ayr Street. Drawn instantly to the charms of Ewelme Cottage, Carolyn was disappointed to hear that she would be exploring the interior of Kinder House in search of itsshadowy apparitions. Michael, on the other hand, was delighted to be able to commune with the shy and gentle spirits of Ewelme Cottage, getting in touch 'with his feminine side!'

Carolyn began her nocturnal exploration of Kinder House in the back gallery rooms, ordered and uncluttered and filled with paintings and photographs taken by John Kinder. Of all the rooms in Kinder House she investigated, the study filled Carolyn with the most trepidation. This room, currently serving as an office for the Kinder House Society, is undergoing renovation. The sloping wooden beams of the ceiling are exposed, the wallpaper is peeling and the room has a damp, musty smell. The room also houses a trapdoor which leads to a small underground cellar.

The light-coloured blur adrift in a field of darkness in the Kinder House cellar has definite facial features.

Naturally, Carolyn was terrified when asked to lift the trapdoor and take a photograph. Images of spiders, buried corpses and psycho-killers flashed before her eyes and it took a great deal of cajoling to convince Carolyn to fulfil her role as a paranormal investigator. The effort was worthwhile, however, and Carolyn's photograph revealed a white blur afloat in the sea of darkness. On closer inspection, the white area has definite facial characteristics, leading to speculation that there was a ghostly entity lurking beneath Kinder House that night.

Down the road in Ewelme Cottage, Michael sensed a presence in the upstairs attic. After taking several photographs and a temperature reading, he paused to evoke the spirit of the little girl that Justine had talked about earlier, inviting her to communicate with him. Then, squatting on his haunches, Michael experienced what he described as a 'cold wave' rushing over him, a force so powerful that it almost knocked him to his feet. Despite the impact, Michael did not feel that it was a negative sensation, rather that it was the spirit announcing its presence. He emerged from the experience with a concrete impression that Ewelme Cottage is indeed haunted.